First Printed in 2021

Published in 2023 by We Love Learning Ltd

Registered at: Warren Court, Park Road, Crowborough, East Sussex TN6 2QX.

Copyright © 2023 by The Learning Lady

ISBN: 978-13999-6276-6

All rights reserved.

No part of this publication may be reproduced in any form or by any means- photographic, digital, or mechanical, without prior written permission from the author.

super sounds

super sounds

The VERY BEST Prephonics Programme

To use with Preschool and Nursery children

The perfect foundation for 2,3- and 4-year old's before **ANY Phonics programme**

@learninglady

*For Molly,
Kitty and Lottie xx*

WELCOME to
super sounds

THE Very Best Prephonic Programme for Preschool and Nursery aged children

Whether you're a nursery teacher, preschool practitioner, childminder, or parent, there really is something in **Super Sounds for everyone**!

Super Sounds is a **super fun and active** preschool phonics programme, preparing children spectacularly well in the lead up to **ANY Phonics Programme.**

It's fully aligned with the expectations of the Early Years Foundation Stage and **best early years practice across the globe.**

super sounds is already achieving AMAZING RESULTS in schools and settings just like yours because it makes **preparing for Phonics fun!**

Super Sounds is **jam-packed** with **fresh inspiration**. You and your **children will LOVE** joining in with the group games, stories, songs, and rhymes, **perfectly picked for 2,3- and 4-year old's.**

Activities are **simple** and **easy** to resource, designed with limited money and time in mind. **super sounds saves** early years educators **BAGS OF TIME!**

Can I use Super Sounds before ANY Phonics Programme?

YES!

super sounds @learninglady

WELCOME to super sounds

There is no expectation that letters and sounds should be introduced to children before they begin school. The pre-phonics learning and development taught using Super Sounds is the **foundation for ANY approach to teaching Phonics.**

Children lacking these **critical prephonic learning experiences** have less success when formal phonics teaching is introduced.
Super Sounds activities are the **essential first step to success in reading.**

Should we use Super Sounds instead of Phase 1 Phonics?

If you've been using Letters and Sounds Phase 1, you'll recognise key similarities with this approach.

But there are a few big differences!

Super Sounds provides a simple but **essential prephonic progression.** It's a more systematic way of teaching pre-phonic learning, helping children to build critical knowledge and skills, step by step.

Repetition is baked into the simple **super sounds** structure. Many of the same games can be played at different points along the prephonic journey, achieving increasingly challenging learning as children develop. This **reduces the complexity of learning** new games at the same time as **developing new skills**.

Stories, songs, and rhymes are the bedrock of **super sounds SUCCESS**! These provide **vital context for the games and activities, making these more relatable to the children.**

Can this structured approach
still be fun and flexible?

Will Super Sounds reduce planning time?

Is this a resource
that's easy to share with colleagues?

YES!

And this book shows you how :)

About the Author

Hello, my name's Emma 'The Learning Lady'!

I've been an Early Years trainer, advisor and former Early Years Ofsted Inspector for more than a decade, and I've been working with 2-5 year old's for more than a quarter of a century! I'm a devoted auntie to three amazing girls, beginner horse rider and am obsessive about getting early learning right for generations to come.

I wrote **super sounds** during the Covid pandemic while I was teaching in an inner-city nursery class. My day-to-day work in educational improvement work was limited, and those three-year old's were so **inspirational**!

Up until then I'd been demonstrating the **activities, songs, and stories** in this book at training events and conferences for years.

Professionals were increasingly bored with the same old **Letters and Sounds Phase 1** games, and I had constantly been asked….

"Do you have a book with all of these new games in?"

"Do you have a recommended booklist for preschool phonics?"

"Could you sing that song again, I didn't quite get the words written down!"

super sounds

There had never been time to get any of this stuff down on paper. Not until the dark days of the pandemic that is, then there was plenty!

I was on a **MISSION** to create a **fun-filled, one-stop shop of inspiration** for anyone working with 2, 3 and 4 year old's, and I had a checklist!

Slowly, day by day, Super Sounds was created. The characters, the progression, the book recommendations, the songs, and the You Tube videos, all slowly developed over time.

And I have been OVERWHELMED and DELIGHTED by its success!

I'm so grateful for the viewers and subscribers to the YouTube Channel and for the positive comments that I receive every day. I love to hear the stories about the games children enjoy and what they've been up to in response to their Super Sounds sessions.

Nowadays I am out and about **sharing the super sounds message EVERYWHERE!** I work with schools, nursery chains and Local Authorities across the UK and the world. I've met some amazing educators and children who are a continued source of inspiration.

I've written articles, blogs, and appeared on podcasts, and was thrilled when Super Sounds became a Teach Early Years finalist in 2022.

And today, I'm HERE JUST FOR YOU!

I'm delighted to be taking you step by step along the Super Sounds journey.

I know that the best part of your job is being with the children, so I really hope Super Sounds provides you (and them) with hours of fun, laughter, learning and reassurance, without the endless planning, preparation, and paperwork.

Remember, you're a super sounds Superhero!

Thanks for everything you do :)

FREE Thank You

to start your Super Sounds Journey!

As a special '**thank you**' for buying Super Sounds, we've got a **FREE bonus booklet** for you to **download straight away!**

There's **heaps of free stuff** here for instant Super Sounds success and to make Super Sounds sessions **even easier** to run!

Check out what's inside for FREE NOW!

Download your **FREE Super Sounds Bonus Booklet** Now at
www.learninglady.co.uk/super-sounds-bonus-booklet

@learninglady

Lets' get off to a flying start by sharing everything that Super Sounds has to offer!

Super Sounds isn't just a book, it's designed to be INTERACTIVE!
Because **your time** is precious, we've put **everything you need** in one place!

Resources are instantly at your fingertips!

With each activity you'll find **quality book recommendations** and **live song streaming** with easy-to-use QR codes.
Save yourself HOURS of scrolling and endless research. Simply scan the QR codes to **access everything you need straight away!**

Intentionally light on resourcing

Everyday objects are generally recommended as an alternative to printed pictures and worksheets. This supports those at the **early stages of language development** and helps young children to **apply their new learning more easily.**

This is good news for grown-ups too! Using everyday 'stuff' **costs less**, is **better for the environment**, and **saves you hours** of preparation time too.

Sharing is Caring

You'll find instantly available **Super Sounds videos** for many activities in this book. These bring the games to life with interactive explanations and **quick demonstrations**, brilliant **for sharing with your team**. They're also great for **sharing with families too!**

14

super sounds

Where to start for Instant Super Sounds Success?

We know that **children are unique**, as are the schools, settings and childminders that support them.
Super Sounds has been written with you in mind.

There's no right way to use this book, **choose whichever way suits your children best** :)

We want you to be able to deliver your sessions with ease and have **hours of fun learning with your children.**

Finding your way around

A Programme in 2 Parts

Part 1: Super Sounds Activities
These are organised according to the 6 step super sounds Success Map outlined on the following pages.
Some professionals use this as a 'dip in, dip out' **resource for activity ideas**, others love more structure so follow these using the planning.

Part 2: Super Sounds Planning Options
There are planning options included for different age groups and session lengths, pick whichever will work best for you to **save yourself hours**. Or use this simple framework to design your own bespoke prephonic curriculum.

@learninglady

Super Simple

Your Super Sounds Journey Starts Here!

Children only secure new learning when it **builds upon prior learning and experiences**, that's why a **firm prephonic foundation is critical** for our 2, 3-, and 4-year-olds.

Prephonic development, or the skills children need to be successful in Phonics, develop through a **graduated process.**

If gaps in this development exist, learning to read using phonics can be more challenging than it needs to be.

Sometimes we can feel pressure to rush ahead, teaching letter names and letter sounds because these are the most obvious parts of this process. But these are only the tip of the iceberg. Learning the basic correspondences between letters and sounds is simply a question of memory and there's much more to preparing our readers than that.

Phonics is a MARATHON and not a sprint!

Pre-Phonic Progression	Auditory Discrimination and Memory Recognise, remember and talk about the similarities and differences in… The sounds what we hear The sounds that we say	Visual Discrimination and Memory Recognise, remember and talk about the similarities and differences in… The shapes that we see		Key Reading Behaviours	Vocabulary
Listening and Attention	Familiar Sounds Musical Sounds	Matching familiar shape/object Copying and matching noises and sounds		Handle books with care, engage in storytelling/music making activities	Developing the language of Naming Describing Reasoning
Phonological Awareness	Rhythm, beat and movement	Copying, matching and sequencing patterns of actions and sounds matched to visual images		Join in with stories songs and rhymes and can turn the pages from front to back	
	Rhyme				
Phonemic Awareness	Alliteration	Reading and recognise the letters in own name and in other situations Creating own patterns and symbols matched to words and actions		Find the beginning, end in a book and talk about a known story	
	Oral blending / Oral segmenting				
Early Reading	Blending / Segmenting	Recognising Letter-sound correspondences	Recognising some common exception words	Pointing to words with 1-1 correspondence	

The skills listed here are less obvious, and arguably more challenging and time consuming to achieve. **A successful prephonic progression** therefore requires a more **thorough and systematic approach**, leaving nothing to chance.

Young children need to be listening, looking, remembering, matching, copying, sorting, and explaining their understanding at every step along this journey. **This ensures that prephonic skills and learning become embedded to build on later.**

For even more information about the pre-phonics journey,
this free training video includes the essentials you need to get started

@learninglady

learninglady.co.uk/get-started-with-super-sounds

Watch on YouTube

Success Made Simple

Here's your Super Sounds success map! A super simple six step prephonic progression that's super easy to follow.

Step 6
Let's learn to hear to hear and say separate sounds in words, ready for making and reading words when school starts

Step 5
Let's learn to hear the similarities and differences in spoken sounds at the start of words

Step 4
Let's learn to break spoken words into chunks by hearing, copying and making rhymes

Step 3
Let's learn to break words into syllables by playing with rhythm

Step 2
Let's learn to make, match and copy lots of sounds with our voices and bodies

Step 1
Let's learn to make, match and copy everyday sounds

At each step along the prephonic journey, your preschoolers will be taught to **differentiate between sounds and symbols.** They'll remember what they see and hear through repetitive memory building games, and they'll be learning the **meaning and pronunciation of new words** to articulate what they're learning too.

TOP TIPS FOR SUPER SOUNDS SUCCESS

⭐
Where to play

Always play Super Sounds games and activities in a quiet, distraction free space.

If we want the children to listen carefully and concentrate well, we need to provide conditions which will make sure this happens.

⭐
Who to play with?

Some games outlined in Super Sounds work best in small groups of no more than 6 children.

These could include children at different stages of development, or you could choose to work with children at similar developmental stages.

Consider which will work best with your current children, being mindful to mix up groupings from time to time for the best results.

⭐
Teaching in larger groups?

Super Sounds activities usually incorporate a story, song, or rhyme because this helps the children by providing a fun context for learning. These are mass participation events! We want the children to be joining in with making sounds, repeating phrases, copying, and offering ideas as much as possible. No hands up and lots of joining in.

Play the games on repeat!

Young children often get lost in the explanation of new games, so we need to keep what we say to a minimum.

Playing the same games in different ways reduces overwhelm and helps the children to focus on the learning you're aiming to achieve.

Organising the children

All Super Sounds small group activities work best with the children sitting in a rainbow shape. This is important because they need to see what you are doing, and you need to be able see how they are getting on.

Sitting in a circle means that some children will not be able to see as well as others and sitting in a group means that some children can become more easily distracted.

Contents

Part 1: The Super Sounds Activities 04

LISTENING AND ATTENTION SKILLS

★ **Step 1** 23
Let's learn to make, match and copy everyday sounds

★ **Step 2** 73
Let's learn to make, match and copy lots of sounds with our voices and bodies

DEVELOPING PHONOLOGICAL AWARENESS

★ **Step 3** 91
Let's learn to break words into syllables by playing with rhythm

★ **Step 4** 113
Let's learn to break spoken words into chunks by hearing, copying, and making rhymes

PHONEMIC AWARENESS: THE PERFECT SPRINGBOARD TO PHONICS

★ **Step 5** 125
Let's learn to hear the similarities and differences in spoken sounds at the start of words

★ **Step 6** 145
Let's learn to hear and say separate sounds in words, ready for making and reading words when school starts

Part 2: Super Sounds Super Plans 163

super sounds

Step 1

Let's learn to make, match and copy everyday sounds

PASS THE BOX

The children will be preparing for phonics by
* Making sounds
* Matching sounds to objects

What you need
* A box
* Toys or objects matched to the sounds you want the children to make
* For example: Farm Animals, Jungle Animals, Vehicles
* You could use pictures or photos if you don't have the toys

How to Play

1. Explain that the children are going to be playing a game by making noises matched to the objects.

2. Show the children each of the toys / pictures you'll be using for the game.

3. Name them and make their sounds all together. Put the toys or pictures into the box.

4. Explain that the children are going to be singing a song to begin the game.

5. As they sing, the children pass the box around the group. At the end of the song, the child holding the box will look inside the box.

Pass The Box Song

🎵

Pass, Pass, Pass the box,
Pass the box around.
When it stops, take a look,
Can you make the sound?
Sung to the tune of row row row your boat

Sing along with instant streaming!

6. The child holding the box should peep inside, choosing a toy.

7. This child shouldn't take the toy out of the box or tell the children which one they have chosen. Instead, this child will give the other children a sound clue for the children to guess which toy they have picked.

8. For example: "choo choo" for the train, "mooooo" for the cow. This will need modelling by an adult first.

9. The other children in the group should guess the toy.

10. The child with the box can reveal whether they were right by holding up the toy as all the children to make the sound again, all together.

11. Repeat the game multiple times by singing the song, passing the box, and encouraging the children to make/ guess the sounds for further toys in the box.

@learninglady

PASS THE BOX

💡 Top Tip

For children at an early stage of vocabulary development, play the game with only 1-2 objects in the box

Keep Playing!

* Turn this into a musical game by using instruments rather than toys.

* Turn this into a rhyming game, with children guessing the object from rhyming clues.

* Turn this into an oral blending and segmenting game by adding simple objects for children to blend orally when the child with the box offers a segmented word clue.

Watch This Game on YouTube

www.learninglady.co.uk/pass-the-box-game

A great book to read with this game!

Noisy Farm by Rod Campbell

NOISY DICE GAME

The children will be preparing for phonics by
* Hearing and matching sounds
* Making sounds

What you need
* A foam die with blank pockets
* or a cube to stick pictures onto to turn into a die, or a homemade cube die made from card
* Pictures of the sound making objects you're going to be playing with. These need to be the same size as the faces / pockets on the die.

What to do

1. Explain that the children are going to make the noises matched to the pictures on the die.

2. Support them to take it in turns to roll the die, naming the picture that lands on top.

3. Can the children name the picture and remember the sounds / actions?

4. All the children should join in with making the sounds / actions to match the picture rolled.

super sounds

5. Be sure to model key vocabulary as different pictures. For example:
"Can you snap like a crocodile?"
"Can you trumpet like an elephant?"
"Can you hiss like a snake."

6. The game continues until everyone in the group has rolled the die at least twice.

> 💡 **TRY THIS**
>
> Use pictures such as farm animal, jungle animals, vehicles, different dinosaurs, aliens, or musical instruments

Keep Playing!

* Turn this into a rhythmic game by clapping the number of syllables in the picture rolled.

* Turn this into a rhyming game by rolling two dice to find a rhyming pair.
  www.learninglady.co.uk/noisy-dice-rhyming-game

* Turn this into an alliteration game by rolling two pictures beginning with the same spoken sound.
  www.learninglady.co.uk/noisy-dice-alliteration-game

* Turn this into an oral blending and segmenting game by rolling simple objects to segment aloud.

@learninglady

31

NOISY DICE GAME

Watch This Game on YouTube

www.learninglady.co.uk/noisy-dice-game

A great book to read with this game!

Dear Zoo by Rod Campbell

super sounds

LISTEN TO THE SHOPPING GAME

step 1

The children will be preparing for phonics by

* Hearing and matching sounds
* Remembering and describing sounds

What you need

* A large shopping bag or shopping basket
* Noise making items
  For example: a packet of crisps to crunch, some keys to rattle, opening a bottle of fizzy drink, a packet of cereal to shake, some coins in a purse to jingle, a mobile phone with a familiar ring tone. Try and find as many different sounding everyday items as you can.
* Use a device to take pictures of the objects to support children with limited vocabularies or less confidence.

HOW TO PLAY

1. Talk with the children about their experiences of going shopping and what they have seen at the shops.

2. Show the children the objects that will be going into the shopping bag.

3. Model using the objects to make the noises, demonstrating how to describe them as you put each into the shopping bag.
   For example: "In goes the cereal, that makes a shaking sound, in goes the fizzy drink, that makes a fizzing sound."

@learninglady

LISTEN TO THE SHOPPING GAME

4. Explain that the children are going to play a guessing game just by listening. They will need to sit quietly and listen carefully so that they can hear the sounds.

Sing the shopping bag song all together:

🎵

Listen to the shopping, what's that sound?
Guess what shopping I have found.
Listen very carefully with your ears,
What's that noise what will you hear?

Sung to the tune of I'm a little teapot

Sing along with instant streaming!

5. Make a noise with one of the objects inside the bag- choose the loudest / most obvious sound first.

6. What can the children hear? Can they name the object? Can they describe the sound?

7. Can they say why they think it is that object? Encourage the use of descriptive sentences by building on what the children say.
For example: "You think it's the crisps because they sound crunchy. "You think it's the lemonade because it sounds fizzy."

super sounds

8. If the children are struggling to name the object, you could show them the photos of the objects to give then some options.

9. Perform a big reveal by taking the sound making object out of the bag. Let the children take it in turns to make the sounds themselves using the shopping item, modelling the language as they make the sounds. For example: "The lemonade makes a fizzing sound."

10. Repeat the game until all the sounds have been guessed.

💡 TOP TIP

Begin with sounds which sound very different, building up to listening out for the differences in more similar sounds

Watch This Game on YouTube

LISTEN TO THE SHOPPPING GAME

www.learninglady.co.uk/shopping-bag-game

A great book to read with this game!

The Shopping List
by John Burningham

NOISY EGGS

step 1

The children will be preparing for phonics by

* Hearing similarities and differences in sounds
* Remembering sounds
* Describing sounds

What you need

* Plastic fillable eggs
* Noise making materials to go inside the eggs
  For example: rice, buttons, old coins, pasta, bells, lentils paperclips.
* Before beginning the game, you'll need to prepare the eggs into pairs that make the same sound, using the sound making materials.
* Split the pairs of eggs and hide one egg from each pair somewhere around the room.

How to Play

1. Explain that the children are going to be finding pairs of eggs that sound the same by shaking and listening.

2. Give each child an egg, with time to shake and listen to the sound. Model describing the sounds they hear.
   "That blue egg is making a jingling sound."
   "This blue egg is making a rattling sound."

@learninglady

37

NOISY EGGS

3. Give the children time to hunt for the matching egg to the one they have been given by shaking found eggs to decide if they sound the same.

4. The game ends when all the eggs have been matched. Check the eggs all together. Have any eggs been mismatched? Model the language again to further develop understanding.

💡 TOP TIP

Start with very different sounding items in the eggs, becoming increasingly similar as children tune in more to the similarities in sounds.

Watch This Game on YouTube

Fun Preschool Listening Game

super sounds

www.learninglady.co.uk/noisy-eggs

A great book to read with this game!

The Odd Egg by Emily Gravett

MUSICAL SOUNDS

step 1

The children will be preparing for phonics by

* Hearing and matching sounds
* Making sounds

What you need

* Two large toys (matched to familiar sounds) placed at either end of a large space, these need to be large enough for the children to see them. For example: a large toy horse and a large toy sheep.
* Alternatively, you could use two large pictures of sound making animals or objects
* A speaker with some music to dance to
* A noisy book with sound effects
  or sound effects downloaded to play through the speaker
  or make your own sound effects!

How to Play

1. Show the children the sound making objects or pictures at either end of the room. Play the sound effects to match the objects.

2. Can the children name the objects and match these with the corresponding sounds?

3. This game is similar to a traditional game of musical statues.

super sounds

4. Explain that the children are going to dance to the music in the middle of the large space.

5. When the music stops, the children need to listen to the sound effect and run to the corresponding object / picture.

6. Play the music. Stop the music. Play / make the sound effect.

7. Once the children have run to the corresponding object or picture, replay the sound effect to check that they matched the sound top the object correctly.

8. The children then return to the center of the space and play continues in this way several times.

💡 TOP TIP

Start with 2 sound making objects, building up to 4 different objects in the corners of the space.
Try this game with farm animals, jungle animals, vehicles, different sounds matched to aliens and other everyday sounds

Watch This Game on YouTube

@learninglady

41

MUSICAL SOUNDS

www.learninglady.co.uk/musical-sounds

Keep playing

✱ Turn this into a musical game by using instruments rather than toys.

✱ Turn this into a rhyming game, with children running to the object matched to the rhyming clues.

✱ Turn this into an oral blending and segmenting game by providing simple objects for children to run to as they blend in their heads from an orally segmented clue.

THE DRUMMER'S IN THE RING

step 1

The children will be preparing for phonics by
* Making and describing differences in sounds

What you need
* A drum placed in the center of the space.
* Children's names / names with photos, handwritten or printed. These should be placed face down around the drum.

How to Play

1. Explain that the children are going to take it in turns the be the drummer. Each child can choose to play the drum loudly or quietly.

2. Model playing the drum in different ways, modelling the language to describe your playing using a full sentence.

3. "I can play the drum loudly", "I can play the drum quietly".

4. Sing the 'Drummer's in the ring 'song all together, encouraging the children to join in with the singing and clapping along in time with the singing.

@learninglady

THE DRUMMER'S IN THE RING

Drummer's in the Ring Song

♫

The drummer's in the ring,
The drummer's in the ring,
Is she loud or is she quiet?
The drummer's in the ring.

Sing to the tune of The Farmers in his den

Sing along with instant streaming!

5. When the singing stops, turn over one of the name cards to choose the first drummer.

6. They are invited into the center of the space to be the drummer during the next verse.

7. Begin singing the song again, with all the children joining in all together, clapping a steady beat.
   As the children sing, the 'drummer' should play the drum loudly / quietly.

8. Can the children guess how the drummer was playing? Loudly? Quietly?

9. When the song ends the drummer can turn over a new name card to choose the next drummer as they rejoin the group.

super sounds

10. Continue in this way until all the children have had a turn.

11. Mix things up by playing the game with fast and slow sounds instead.

Watch This Game on YouTube

www.learninglady.co.uk/drummer-in-the-ring

CHOOSE A SOUND SONG

step 1

The children will be preparing for phonics by
* Listening to, and describing, differences in sounds
* Matching words with objects

What you need
* A selection of familiar musical instruments placed in the center of the space, enough for 1 per child. These could be real or homemade sound makers.
* A bag containing the children's names/ names with photos.

How to Play

1. Explain that the children are going to be musicians, taking turns to choose an instrument from those in the center of the space.

2. Show the children the bag with the names inside. Read each of the names all together, using the photos as a support if necessary.

3. Explain that the children are going to pass the bag around the group as the children sing a song.

super sounds

♪
"Choose the sound you will play,
You will play, you will play.
Choose the sound you will play,
What's your favourite?'

*Sung to the tune of
London Bridge is Falling Down*

Sing along with instant streaming!

4. Encourage the children to join in with the singing as much as possible, clapping the beat as the bag is passed.

5. As the singing ends, the child holding the bag should look to find their name.

6. They should choose an instrument.

7. For more developed talkers, encourage them to say why a particular instrument has been chosen.

8. "I like the drum because it's loud", "I like the bells, they sound like Santa".

9. Sing the song all together again, passing the bag and clapping as before.

10. The child with the instrument can play along as everyone sings.

CHOOSE A SOUND SONG

11. Repeat the singing, selecting, naming, and playing of the musical instruments until all the children are playing their instruments, and there are no more names in the bag.

TRAFFIC LIGHTS GAME

step 1

The children will be preparing for phonics by

* Listening to, and making, sounds of differing speeds
* Matching sounds with symbols

What you need

* Instruments or homemade sound makers (enough for 1 per child)
* Traffic lights- you can draw these onto a large sheet of paper or create a slide.

How to Play

1. Introduce the traffic lights. Do the children know what happens when they see the different colours on the traffic lights?

2. Explain that the children are going to use the instruments to play in a way that matches the colours on the traffic lights.

3. Model the process by pointing to the green light, playing one of the instruments as quickly as possible.

4. Point to the amber light, playing the instrument much more slowly.

@learninglady

49

5. Point to the red light and stop playing.

6. Practise this with the children using their own instruments all together.

7. Play the game by trying to catch the children out, pointing to the different coloured lights out of sequence with growing speed as the children grow in confidence.

Watch This Game on YouTube

www.learninglady.co.uk/traffic-lights-game

SUPER SOUND SEQUENCES

step 1

The children will be preparing for phonics by

* Matching sounds to symbols
* Remembering sounds in sequence

What you need

* A range of musical instruments
* Photos of the instruments organised into simple sequences and printed out for the children to see. These could be pasted onto strips of paper or slides for larger group work. Alternatively, you could draw your own, making sure your pictures match the real instruments as far as possible.
* Example patterns might include:
* Tambourine, tambourine, drum, tambourine, tambourine, drum
* Maracas, bells, maracas, maracas, bells, maracas, bells, maracas, maracas, bells

How to Play

1. Share each of the instruments you'll be using for the game. Practise naming the instruments all together, listening to the special features of each instrument.

2. Model a description of each sound.
   "This is the drum; it makes a loud banging sound."
   "This is the tambourine; it makes a rattling sound".

3. With all the instruments organised into the middle of the space, explain that the children are going to be musicians using the picture patterns to guide them.

@learninglady

SUPER SOUNDS SEQUENCES

4. Demonstrate playing one of the simple patterns using the instruments, saying the names of the instruments as a model.

5. Involve the children in saying the sequence several times all together. Show them how to follow the picture pattern, by pointing to the pictures in order. This helps the children to become aware that the directionality of print in English goes from left to right.

6. "Tambourine, drum, tambourine, drum, tambourine, drum, tambourine drum."

7. Share out the instruments, explaining that the children will only play their instrument when the corresponding picture is being pointed to.

8. When a different instrument is being pointed to, they must hold their own instrument still until it is their turn in the pattern again.

9. Always start with simple two-part sequences, becoming more complex overtime. Begin by using instruments which sound very different, using more similar sounding instruments over time.

> 💡 **TOP TIP**
>
> Help the children to create and play their own musical patterns by printing out more copies of the photos / images, mounting them onto Velcro or with adhesive putty (like Blu Tac) to create changeable patterns and simple compositions.

Keep Playing!

* Make new sound patterns using animal sounds, vehicle sounds or crazy alien noises.

Watch This Game on YouTube

www.learninglady.co.uk/sound-sequences

MUSICAL HIDE AND SEEK

step 1

The children will be preparing for phonics by
* Changing and describing sounds
* Matching sounds to actions

What you need
* Instruments or homemade sound makers (enough for 1 per child)
* An object to hide and seek (for example a favourite toy)
* A blindfold (optional)

How to Play

1. Explain that the children are going to play a game of musical hide and seek, using the instruments to give clues.

2. Introduce the concept of playing the instruments to provide the clues by placing the object that will be hiding in the center of the space.

3. Encourage the children to play the musical instruments, becoming louder as you move nearer to the object.

4. The further away you move from the object, the children should play their instruments increasingly quietly. Practise this all together first.

5. Introduce the game using one of the children or a second adult as a model. They will need to hide their eyes, possibly using the blindfold.

super sounds

6. Hide the chosen object so that the remaining children can see where the object is, without telling the blindfolded child / adult.

7. Remove the blindfold or ask the adult / child to uncover their eyes. This person is then tasked with finding the object using the musical clues provided by the remaining children, just like in a traditional game of hide and seek.

8. Guide the children to play the musical instruments more quietly as the adult / child moves further away from the object, more loudly as he / she is nearer to the object.

9. The aim of the game is to guide the adult / child to find the hidden object, playing the musical clues louder and more quietly all together.

10. Once the object has been found, repeat the activity with further children seeking the hidden object.

Keep playing

* Once the children have mastered the difference between loud and quiet sounds, play the game with fast and slow sound clues instead.

NOISY ANIMALS

step 1

The children will be preparing for phonics by

* Hearing and making sounds
* Listening and matching sounds

What you need

* Toy farm animals: depending on the number of children playing you'll need several of each type. You could use pictures or photos of the animals if you don't have enough animals for everyone.
* A bag; place the animals in the bag
* A large space to play

What To Do

1. Explain that the children are going to pretend to be farm animals by making the animal sounds matched to the toys or pictures.

2. Practise by pulling each animal out of the bag. Make the matching noise for each animal all together.

3. Explain that the children are each going to take their own animal out of the bag and think about the noise it makes. Then they are going to hide the animal away in their hand so nobody else can see it. Model and practise this first.

4. On your signal, the children move around the space, making the noise of their animal without showing anybody the toy or picture they have in their hands.

super sounds

5. The aim of the game is to find, then stand with, the animals making the same sound, without showing the other children which animal they are holding.

6. Support the children in making the animal sounds at the same time as moving around the space. As well as making their own animal sounds, they will need to be listening out for the animals which are the same as them.

7. Once all the 'animals' have organised themselves into groups, ask each group of children to make their sounds once more. revealing the toys or pictures to check that they were right.

💡 **TOP TIP**

This is best played in a larger group of at least 10 children.

Keep Playing!

* You can play this game with jungle animals, vehicles or even aliens that make different sounds!

A great book to read with this game!

Farmer Duck by Martin Waddell

@learninglady

WHICH ANIMAL IS HIDING?

step 1

The children will be preparing for phonics by

* Making sounds
* Matching sounds to objects
* Remembering sounds

What you need

* A collection of 6 farm animal toys or pictures
* Toys could include a cow, a horse, a sheep, a pig, a dog, a cat, a duck, a hen
* Printed photos of each toy
* A box with one of the toy animals added

How To Play

1. Arrange the photos of the animals in front of children. Practise naming and making the sounds for these animals, all together.

2. Explain that one of the animals is hiding in the box, and the children will be guessing which it is using some sound clues.

3. Begin by giving the first clue.

4. "The animal that's hiding doesn't make a "baaaa" sound".

5. Encourage the children to identify the sound with the matching picture, turning it over to discount this animal.

6. The children will need some help to realise that this isn't the animal that's hiding in the box.

super sounds

7. Continue with further clues.

8. "The animal that's hiding doesn't make a "woof" sound. As before, support the children by matching the animal with the corresponding sound, turning over the corresponding image.

9. Continue in this way until only 1 picture is remaining.

10. Can the children name and make the sound for the animal? Is this the animal that's hiding?

11. Reveal the animal hiding in the box. Did the children guess the missing animal using the sound clues?

12. Repeat with further animals and challenge some children to give the clues themselves as they gain confidence.

A great book to read with this game!

The Farmer's Away, Baa, Neigh by Anne Vittur Kennedy

WHO'S AT THE DOOR?

step 1

The children will be preparing for phonics by
* Hearing and matching sounds
* Remembering sounds

What you need
* This is a game requiring 2 adults. 1 adult will be leading the game, 1 adult will become the characters at the door.
* Simple costume props for, or pictures of, the characters knocking at the door (Optional). These should be characters the children are familiar with.

How To Play

1. Explain that there will be different characters coming to see them. They will be knocking on the door and making a sound clue for the children to work out who they are.

2. **Adult 2**
   Knocks loudly on the door or from behind a barrier (like a cupboard).

3. **Adult 1**
   Model and encourages the children to join in with singing the song

super sounds

> "Who is knocking at the door,
> at the door, at the door.
> Who is knocking at the door,
> Can you hear them?"
>
> *Sung to the tune of
> London Bridge is Falling Down*

Sing along with instant streaming!

4. **Adult 1**

   Guide the game by asking Adult 2 to give the children a clue to help them work out who it might be.

5. **Adult 2**

   Make a sound matched to a chosen character.
   This could include:
   Father Christmas, "*Ho, Ho Ho*" and the jingling of some bells
   The Giant from Jack and the Beanstalk, "*Fi, Fi Fo Fum*" and stamping in giant boots.
   A Pirate "*A hah me hearties*" and a parrot squawking

6. **Adult 1**

   Which character could be behind the door, based on the sound clues? Can children with more developed vocabularies explain their thinking using the sentence starter:
   "I think it could be …. because…."

WHO'S AT THE DOOR?

7. Adult 2

Reveal the character. Did the children guess the character correctly?

8. Repeat with further characters, with children in role behind the door as they grown in confidence.

A great book to read with this game!

Knock Knock, Who's There?
by Sally Grindley and Anthony Browne

SANTA'S SECRET PRESENTS

step 1

The children will be preparing for phonics by

* Hearing similarities and differences in sounds
* Remembering and matching sounds
* Describing sounds

What you need

* 10 or more recycled boxes; cereal boxes, shoes boxes, match boxes. You need an even number, ideally these should be a mixture of shapes and sizes.
* Sound making items to go inside the boxes; rice, buttons, old coins, pasta, bells, lentils or paperclips are all good to use.
* Wrapping paper to wrap the boxes.
* A Santa's sack to keep the boxes and Santa hats to play in role (optional)
* Prepare for the game by filling pairs of boxes with the same sound making materials.
  For example: two boxes containing the same amount of rice, two boxes containing the same number of lentils etc.
* When all the boxes have been filled, wrap them using the wrapping paper.

How To Play

1. Explain that Santa's elves have muddled the presents in the workshop, and they are all mixed up inside the sack. Santa needs the children to help organise the presents into matching pairs. They won't be able to do this by looking, they must do this by listening.

@learninglady

63

SANTA'S SECRET PRESENTS

2. Support the children to take it in turns, listening very carefully.

3. The first child takes two presents from the sack, giving them a shake to hear the sound inside.

4. The children must decide if the presents sound the same, or if they sound different.

5. If the presents sound the same, both presents can be taken out as a matching pair and set aside. If the presents don't sound the same, they are both returned to the sack.

6. Model vocabulary to describe the sounds as the children shake the presents. For example:
"That's a jingling sound", "That's a rattling sound, "That's a clinking sound".

7. Ask children with more developed vocabularies to describe what they've heard, explaining how the sounds are the same or different.

8. Play continues in this way, with the children taking turns, until all presents have been matched.

9. Following the game, check the sound matching by opening the presents. Were the matching sounds made by the same items?

A great book to read with this game!

Dear Santa by Rod Campbell

THE RING TONE GAME

step 1

The children will be preparing for phonics by

* Hearing differences in sounds
* Remembering and matching sounds
* Describing sounds

What you need

* 2 adults with 2 mobile phones
  (with 2 distinctly different ring tones)
* A large space to play

How To Play

1. Talk with the children about the different types of sounds that they hear in their homes. Can they identify some different everyday sounds? Challenge more confident talkers to describe the sounds they recognise (loud, quiet, fast, slow, ringing, banging etc.)

2. Explain that this listening game uses a familiar sound, the ring tone on a phone. Introduce the concept that ring tones can be different, even though they are doing the same job.

3. Each adult should play the ring tone on their phone for all the children to hear.

4. Hiding the phones, the adults should separately play the ring tones. Encourage the children to point to the adult playing the matching ring tone.

@learninglady

THE RING TONE GAME

5. Explain that the adults are going to stand at either end of the large space, with the children standing in the center.

6. One adult begins by playing a ring tone. On hearing the ring tone, can the children run to the adult playing the matching sound?

7. The adult should replay the ring tone so the children can check that they ran to the matching adult.

8. Ask the children to return to the center of the space and replay the game again.

9. Can the adults catch the children out?

💡 TOP TIP

For more challenge, change the ring tones to more similar sounds so the children listen more carefully. Add further ring tones by adding more adults into the game.

Watch This Game on YouTube

super sounds

www.learninglady.co.uk/ring-tone-game

WHICH INSTRUMENT?

step 1

The children will be preparing for phonics by

* Listening to and remembering sounds
* Identifying and describing the differences between sounds

What you need

* Several instruments making different sounds.
* Create a barrier between you and the children. This needs to be large enough to hide and play the instruments behind. It could be a box, a ring binder, or a piece of card folded into a standing position.
* Printed photos of each of the instruments. Place these in front of the children or stick them onto the outside of the barrier.

How To Play

1. Remind the children of the instrument sounds and names, saying these all together.

2. Explain that the children will be guessing which instrument is being played by listening for the musical clues.

3. Begin by introducing the song for the game.

super sounds

🎵
"I've got sounds,1 (play instrument 1)
and 2 (play instrument 2)"
Show the instruments as you play them.

"Hideaway."
*Hide both instruments
behind the barrier.*

"Listen now, listen now."
"Which shall I play?"
Sing to the tune of Tommy Thumb

Sing along with instant streaming!

4. Play one of the instruments from behind the barrier. Can the children guess the instrument?

5. Encourage children who struggle to name the instrument by pointing to the matching picture.

6. Challenge children who guess which sound is being played to describe how they know.
   For example:
   "The triangle makes a tinging sound."
   "The bells make a jangling sound".

7. Repeat several times then challenge more confident children to take the 'teacher' role, playing the instruments behind the barrier.

WHICH INSTRUMENT?

💡 TOP TIP

For children who are confident at tuning in and spotting similarities in sounds, pick instruments which sound more alike to challenge their listening and attention skills.

You can also use everyday objects too. Try jangling some keys and snipping with some scissors, stirring a spoon in a cup, or shaking a cereal packet.

BIG BAND

step 1

The children will be preparing for phonics by

* Matching actions to symbols and sounds
* Hearing the differences between sounds

What you need

* Musical Instruments- at least enough for one per child (these can be homemade instruments if you don't have enough real ones).
* Place the instruments in a circle, with space between the instruments before beginning. It might be useful to chalk a circle so that children can see where the instruments belong in this game.
* Favourite music and a device to play the music on.

How To Play

1. Explain that the children are going to be musicians and that you are going to be the conductor.

2. Demonstrate some signals that the children will need to follow.

3. Explain that when the children see your hands pointing high above your head, they will need to play the instruments quickly.

4. If your hands are pointing down low towards your toes, the children will need to play slowly.

@learninglady

71

BIG BAND

5. Also agree a 'stopping' signal. On this signal the children will put the instruments back onto the chalked circle.

6. Organise the children to be standing in an outer circle around the instruments. The children need to be facing inwards, holding hands facing the circle of instruments in the center. Once organised, ask the children to release one another's hands, turning in a clockwise direction.

7. Explain that the children are going to follow one another around the circle as some of their favourite music is played. The children will be able to move freely and dance in whatever way they like, but they need to remain in the circle. All the children need to be moving in the same direction.

8. Practise this part of the game first, playing some music, then stopping as soon as the music is paused.

9. Explain that the next time the music is stopped, the children need to grab any instrument from the circle in front of them.

10. Once everyone has an instrument, introduce the hand signals as previously practised.

11. Practise playing quickly and slowly before introducing the stop signal. Wait until all the children have returned the instruments to the chalked circle in the middle and have returned to their original places.

12. Play the music again with the children moving in a clockwise direction as before.

13. Repeat this game several times, stopping and starting the music, collecting, and playing the instruments matched to the signals.

> 💡 **TOP TIP**
>
> A few extra instruments are useful for this game to ensure that the children can focus on the music making, rather than whether there will be enough instruments.

Keep Playing!

* Make this game increasingly more complicated over time by introducing different signals, with more for the children to remember.

A great book to read with this game!

Animal Music by Julia Donaldson and Nick Sharratt

super sounds

Step 2

Let's learn to make, match and copy lots of sounds with our voices and bodies

FEEL THE BEAT

step 2

The children will be preparing for phonics by
* Keeping a steady beat, ready for introducing syllables
* Matching movements to words
* Following simple instructions

What you need
* You don't need anything to join in with this song!

How To Play

1. This is a joining in song, so encourage the children to participate as much as possible with the singing and the actions.

> *This can simply be sung to the tune of Row, Row, Row your boat.*
>
> ♫
> **Sing along with instant streaming!**

2. Make sure the children have enough space between then to move freely and safely.

3. Begin by modelling the first verse for the children.

76

super sounds

Clap clap, clap your hands,
Clap your hands together.
Clap clap, clap your hands,
Clap your hands together.

4. Repeat a few times, encouraging the children to join in with the singing and actions all together.

5. As the children gain confidence repeat with further verses.

Pat, pat, pat, pat your knees,
Pat your knees together.
Pat, pat, pat your knees,
Pat your knees together.

Stomp, stomp, stomp your feet,
Stomp your feet together.
Stomp, stomp, stomp your feet,
Stomp your feet together.

Blink, blink, blink your eyes,
Blink your eyes together.
Blink, blink, blink your eyes,
Blink your eyes together.
Tap, tap, tap your head,

Tap your head together,
Tap, tap, tap your head,
Tap your head together.

Kick, kick, kick your legs,
Kick your legs together.
Kick, kick, kick your legs,
Kick your legs together.

FEEL THE BEAT

Watch This Song on YouTube

www.learninglady.co.uk/feel-the-beat

WADDLE LIKE A PENGUIN

step 2

The children will be preparing for phonics by

* Matching movements to words
* Following simple instructions
* Using their bodies to make different shapes (ready for making letter shapes later)

What you need

* You don't need anything to join in with this song!

How To Play

1. This is a joining in song, so encourage the children to participate as much as possible with the singing and the actions.
Make sure the children have enough space between then to move freely and safely.

This can be sung to the tune of Apples and Bananas.

♪
Sing along with instant streaming!

2. Begin by modelling the first verse for the children.

@learninglady

WADDLE LIKE A PENGUIN

3. Repeat a few times, encouraging the children to join in with the singing and actions all together.

    I like to waddle, waddle, waddle, waddle like a penguin,
    I like to waddle, waddle, waddle, waddle like a penguin.
    I like to waddle, waddle, waddle, waddle like a penguin,
    I like to waddle, waddle, waddle, waddle like a penguin.

4. As the children gain confidence repeat with further verses.

    I like to flap, flap, flap just like an ostrich,
    I like to flap, flap, flap just like an ostrich.
    I like to flap, flap, flap just like an ostrich,
    I like to flap, flap, flap just like an ostrich.

    I like to slither, slither, slither just like a snake,
    I like to slither, slither, slither just like a snake.
    I like to slither, slither, slither just like a snake,
    I like to slither, slither, slither just like a snake.

    I like to stomp, stomp, stomp just like an elephant,
    I like to stomp, stomp, stomp just like an elephant.
    I like to stomp, stomp, stomp just like an elephant,
    I like to stomp, stomp, stomp just like an elephant.

    I like to peck, peck, peck just like a chicken,
    I like to peck, peck, peck just like a chicken.
    I like to peck, peck, peck just like a chicken,
    I like to peck, peck, peck just like a chicken.

    I like to jiggle and wiggle just like a monkey,
    I like to jiggle and wiggle just like a monkey.
    I like to jiggle and wiggle just like a monkey,
    I like to jiggle and wiggle just like a monkey.

5. Can the children think of any more animals (noises / actions) to join in with?

Watch This Song on YouTube

www.learninglady.co.uk/waddle-like-a-penguin

A great book to read with this game!

Doing the Animal Bop by Jan Ormerod

THE PIRATE CAPTAIN SAYS...

step 2

The children will be preparing for phonics by

* Matching movements to words
* Following simple instructions
* Using their bodies to make different shapes (ready for making letter shapes and patterns later)

What you need

* You don't need anything to play this game!
* A pirate hat for the role of Pirate Captain (optional)

How To Play

1. This is a 'piratey' version of the game *Simon Says*.

2. Explain that you are the Pirate Captain, and the children are going to pretend to be the pirates on your ship.

3. The children need to listen very carefully, joining in with actions for the instructions given by the Pirate Captain.

4. Practise some actions all together. These could include:

    * Scrub the floor
    * Hop on 1 leg
    * Swim in the sea
    * Dig for treasure
    * Read your map
    * Keep a lookout
    * Raise the flag
    * Walk the plank
    * Go to bed

super sounds

5. Explain that the pirates (the children) need to beware because the Pirate Captain will try to catch them out by changing the instructions.

6. If an instruction begins with *"Pirate Captain says…."* (followed by the action), the children should complete the action. Just like in a traditional game of Simon Says.

7. If an instruction is given which doesn't begin with *"Pirate Captain says…."* then the children need to freeze and stand as still as possible.

8. Repeat the activity several times, with the pirates listening and responding to Pirate Captain, either by joining in with the actions or standing still.

9. Begin with only two or three different actions, adding more actions as the skills of listening and responding develop.

10. As the children grow in confidence, choose one of them to act in the role of Pirate Captain.

A great book to read with this game!

Go Go Pirate Boat
by Katrina Champman

BUSY BIRDS

step 2

The children will be preparing for phonics by

* Matching movements to words
* Following simple instructions
* Using their bodies to make different shapes (ready for making letter shapes later)

What you need

* A large space to play.
* Fillable plastic eggs which can be split in half (enough for one per child)
* Actions for some different birds (written on paper and placed inside the eggs)
* For example: swoop like a starling, stand on 1 leg like a flamingo, twit twoo like an owl, cock-a-doodle-do like a cockerel, peck like a woodpecker, waddle like a penguin in the snow.
* Hide the plastic eggs containing the actions around the large space for the children to find.
* The Birdie Song (online) and a device to play the music.

How To Play

1. Explain that the birds have been busy laying eggs all around the space, leaving the children some bird clues to find.

2. Begin by playing the music, with the children joining in with the 'birdie' actions.

super sounds

3. While everyone is dancing, choose one of the children to hunt for one egg, explaining that you and the children are going to continue with the music and dancing while they hunt.

4. As soon as 1 egg has been found, pause the music.

5. Ask the child to crack open the plastic egg and reveal a bird action, read it aloud to the group.

6. Encourage all the children to join in with the actions and sounds described in the egg, then play the Birdie Song again.

7. Continue as before, selecting a second child to hunt for the second egg while the children are dancing.

8. Keep playing with the dancing, finding, and acting out the noises / actions, until all eggs have been found.

A great book to read with this game!

A Busy Day for Birds
by Lucy Cousins

ROARING DINOSAURS

step 2

The children will be preparing for phonics by

* Matching movements to words
* Following simple instructions
* Using their bodies to make different shapes (ready for making letter shapes later)

What you need

* You don't need anything to play.

How To Play

1. Introduce the Dinosaur Romp rhyme, saying it aloud and modelling the actions for the children:

♫

"Romping, stomping, romping, stomping"
(Stamping and stomping around the space like a dinosaur)
"Show your pointed claws."
(Show your claws)
"Romping, stomping, romping, stomping"
(Stamping and stomping)
"Give a great bit roar."
(Roar)

2. Encourage the children to join in with the actions and sounds first, then join in with the rhyme as they become more confident.

86

super sounds

A great book to read with this game!

Dinosaur Roar
by Paul and Henrietta Stickland

JIGGLE IN THE JUNGLE!

step 2

The children will be preparing for phonics by

* Matching movements to words
* Following simple instructions
* Using their bodies to make different shapes (ready for making letter shapes later)

What you need

* You don't need anything to play this game.

How To Play

1. Explain that the children are going to be jungle explorers by walking through the jungle together. Which animals will they see?

2. Practise roaring like a tiger, swinging like a monkey, stomping like an elephant, flapping like a bird, leaping like a leopard, slithering like a snake. Encourage the children to join in with the actions as much as possible.

3. Explain that the children are going to play a following the leader game. Whatever action and sound the leader of the line is making, the children in the line behind the leader will need to copy and continue. This is like a traditional game of Following the Leader.

4. Organise the children into a line, beginning with a simple action such as flapping like a bird. Can the children stay in line, following you (the leader) moving through the jungle?

5. Once you can see that the children understand the idea of copying the leader and staying in line, continue with further actions.

6. Continue in this way until the children have practised sounds and actions for lots of different animals by following the leader.

7. As the children grow in confidence, pick different children as new leaders of the line. Encourage the children to add new animals and actions to the game too.

Keep Playing

* Try this with farm animals or different types of dinosaurs too!

A great book to read with this game!

Walking Through the Jungle by Julie Lacome

ALIENS, ALIENS EVERYWHERE!

step 2

The children will be preparing for phonics by

* Making and copying different sounds with their voices
* Matching pictures to voice sounds
* Matching actions to voice sounds

What you need

* A large space to dance and play.
* Some pictures of Aliens (no more than 4). These could be hand drawn or you could use clip art. They need to be large enough for the children to see in the space that you're playing in.
* Alien inspired music and a device to play the music (optional)

How To Play

1. Explain that the children are going to be aliens, making sounds and actions which match the alien pictures.

2. Before playing, make up some alien voice sounds to go with each alien:
   For example:
   "Zaa zee Zaa Zee, Zaa, Zee"
   "Dar Dar Doop, Dar Dar Doop"
   "Bish lish, woosh, bish, lish, woosh"
   "Flim flam, flummy, flim, flam, flummy"

3. Next make up moves to match each alien. Make these as simple or as silly as you like!

super sounds

For example
Shaking your head at the same time as kicking your legs
Creating arm waves and jumping up and down
Running backwards with windmill arms
Wiggling your bottom and clapping

4. Show the children the first alien, modelling the voice sounds and body moves that you've chosen for that alien. Encourage the children to join in by copying the sounds and moves. Repeat with the remaining aliens.

5. Explain that you are going to play some special alien music for the children to move to. While the music is playing, the children will fly around the space in their spaceships. When you pause the music, the children will need to freeze.

6. Practise this so the children get an idea of not bumping into one another, making the most of the space.

7. When the children freeze, they are going to become one of the aliens in the pictures. Hold up one of the alien pictures. Can the children remember and perform the voice sounds and body moves matching the alien in the picture?

8. Model this first by flying your spaceship, freezing, then performing the moves and sounds matched to an alien picture, then join in with the children as they play.

9. Repeat several times, choosing different aliens. Use more complex moves and sounds as the children grow in confidence and memory skills / coordination develop.

ALIENS, ALIENS EVERYWHERE!

Watch This Game on YouTube

www.learninglady.co.uk/noisy-aliens

A great book to read with this game!

There's An Alien In My Book by Tom Fletcher

super sounds

Step 3

Let's learn to break words into syllables by playing with rhythm

PASS THE TAMBOURINE AROUND

step 3

The children will be preparing for phonics by

* Clapping or playing the syllables or beats in words.
* This helps children understand that whole words can be broken down into smaller chunks of sound.

What you need

* A tambourine

How To Play

1. Explain that the children are going to take it in turns to play the tambourine. When it's their turn they are going to use the tambourine to tap out the beats (syllables) in their names.

2. Practise clapping the syllables in some names as an example, with everybody joining in.

3. Remember, the syllables are the 'beats' in words, each syllable or 'beat' is created by a vowel.

For example
"Sam" (1 clap)
"Ash-an" (2 claps)
"Ell-a-Rose" (3 claps)
"Ram-a tou-li" (4 claps)

4. Sing the 'Pass the tambourine song' all together. As they sing, the children pass the tambourine around the group.

super sounds

"Pass the tambourine around,
-rine around, -rine around.
Pass the tambourine around,
Who will play it?

Sing to the tune of London Bridge is falling down

Sing along with instant streaming!

5. As the song ends, one of the children will be holding the tambourine.

6. Encourage this child to tap out the beats (syllables) in their name. Initially, some children will need this modelling, with an adult clapping the beats before they have a go.

7. Encourage the remaining children to echo back the beats in this name by listening then clapping the syllables or 'beats' as you say it.

8. Sing the song again, encouraging participation in the singing and clapping a steady beat as the tambourine is passed.

9. Repeat the same process of tapping out the syllables and passing the instrument until all the children have had a turn.

PASS THE TAMBOURINE AROUND

💡 **TOP TIP**

Clapping the syllables in children's names is something which can be done throughout the day during lots of routine activities where children's names are used for instructions.

Watch This Game on YouTube

www.learninglady.co.uk/pass-the-tambourine-around

COPY MY CLAPS

step 3

The children will be preparing for phonics by
* Hearing, copying and remembering patterns of sound.

What you need
* You don't need anything to play this game.

How To Play

1. This is a simple clapping game, where the children listen to a pattern clapped by an adult, then clap the pattern back like an echo.

2. Before beginning, it's a great idea to think of the patterns you want to use.

3. If you're struggling to think of a range of patterns, i think of categories of objects. For example: types of fruit, animals, transport etc.

4. Once you've picked a category, make a list of words in the category.

5. Work out the number of syllables or 'beats' in each word. The syllables in the words will form the 'claps'.
   For example: in the case of fruit you could use a list like this:
   App-le, pear, app-le, pear, app-le, pear, app-le, pear, app-le, pear, app-le pear, app-le, pear
   Pine-app-le, or-ange, pine-app-le, or-ange, pine-app-le, or-ange, pine-app-le, or-ange, pine-app-le, or-ange
   App-le, app-le, pine-app-le, or-ange, app-le, pine-app-le, or-ange, app-le, pine-app-le, or-ange

@learninglady

COPY MY CLAPS

6. You can choose to use pictures or objects to support the clapping pattern process in the beginning, removing these as the children become more confident at hearing, remembering, and repeating the patterns.

7. Begin with simple two-part patterns, becoming more complex as listening and memory skills develop.

Watch This Game on YouTube

www.learninglady.co.uk/copy-my-claps

LITTLE DRUMMER'S DRUMMING

step 3

The children will be preparing for phonics by

* Clapping or playing the syllables or 'beats' in words. This helps children understand that whole words can be broken down into smaller chunks, ready for reading and spelling later.

What you need

* A drum, placed in the center of the space.

How To Play

1. Begin by clapping the syllables in each child's name all together. The syllables are the 'beats' in words, each syllable or beat is created by a vowel.

   For example
   Jack (1 clap)
   Oscar (2 claps)
   Khadija (3 claps)
   Abdulrahman (4 claps)

2. Model tapping some of the names on the drum too.

3. Choose one of children to be the first drummer. This child should go and sit with the drum in the center of the space.

4. Demonstrate singing this Little Drummer song, encouraging the children to clap a steady beat as you sing.

@learninglady

LITTLE DRUMMER'S DRUMMING

"Molly is the drummer,
Molly is the drummer,
Molly is the drummer,
Let's hear her play her name."

This can be sung to the tune of The bear went over the mountain

Sing along with instant streaming!

5. When the first verse has ended, encourage the child drummer to play their name, by saying it aloud, then tapping the syllables on the drum. For example: Moll-y (2 beats on the drum).

6. Encourage the children without a drum to continue singing the second verse of the Little Drummer song all together.

7. Model then encourage the drummer to play the syllables and say their name aloud at the appropriate points in the song.

For example
"She plays her name like this.
Moll-y (drummer plays 2 drumbeats)
She plays her name like this."
Moll-y (drummer plays 2 drumbeats)

8. Complete the song by repeating the first verse, with all the children keeping a steady beat by clapping, with the drummer tapping a steady beat as before.

> "Molly is the drummer,
> Molly is the drummer,
> Molly is the drummer,
> We heard her play her name."

9. Repeat the process with further drummers, encouraging increased participation as the children grow in confidence.

Watch This Game on YouTube

www.learninglady.co.uk/little-drummers-drumming

WHICH ANIMAL IS HIDING?

step 3

The children will be preparing for phonics by

* Clapping or playing the syllables or 'beats' in words. This helps children understand that whole words can be broken down into smaller chunks, ready for reading and spelling later.

What you need

* Pictures or toy animals. You need a mixture of animals with 1,2,3 and 4 syllable animal names. For example:
Snake or fish (1 syllable)
zeb-ra or li-on (2 syllables)
fla-min-go or cro-co-dile (3 syllables)
cha-me-le-on (4 syllables)
* Remember, the syllables are the 'beats' in words, each syllable or 'beat' is created by a vowel.

How To Play

1. Show the children the animals you've chosen for the game. Pick 1 animal for each number of syllables.
For example: snake (1), zebra (2), crocodile (3), chameleon (4)

2. Checking that the children can name the animals.

3. Practise clapping the beats (syllables) in each of the animals' names all together, several times.
Snake (1 clap), zebra (2 claps), crocodile (3 claps), chameleon (4 claps)

super sounds

4. Explain that you are going to hide all the animals and give a clapping clue. The children need to guess which animal you are clapping.

5. Once the animals are hidden, clap the beats (number of syllables) to match a chosen animal. Can the children guess the animal you are clapping?

6. Support by offering a choice of 2 options to make this more achievable in the beginning.
For example: "Could it be the snake? (1 clap), or the crocodile? (3 claps)."

7. Once the children have decided on an animal, perform a 'big reveal', showing the hidden picture then re-clapping the number of beats (syllables), with the children joining in all together.

8. Repeat with further animals, providing more animal options and reducing support as the children gain confidence and begin to hear the number of syllables for themselves.

> 💡 **TOP TIP**
>
> Use other contexts such as sea life. For example: Crab (1 clap), sea-horse (2 claps), oct-o-pus (3 claps)

Watch This Game on YouTube

@learninglady

105

WHICH ANIMAL IS HIDING?

www.learninglady.co.uk/which-animal-is-hiding

Keep Playing!

* Turn this into a rhyming guessing game by calling out a word which rhymes with one of the animals instead of clapping the syllables.

* Turn this into an oral blending game by calling out the separate spoken sounds in the animals for the children to blend the sounds. Use only 1 syllable words (farm animals are great for this)

A great book to read with this game!

Brown bear, Brown bear, What Do You See? by Eric Carle and Bill Martin Junior

SYLLABLE SCRAMBLE

step 3

The children will be preparing for phonics by

* Clapping or playing the syllables or 'beats' in words. This helps children understand that whole words can be broken down into smaller chunks, ready for reading and spelling later.

What you need

* A large space to play - this is an active game.
* 2 every day or common objects, each with a different number of syllables
* Objects chosen could be made up of 1, 2, or 3 syllables. Here are some everyday examples you could try

1 syllable words	2 syllable words	3 syllable words
Cloth	Tea-towel	Ta-ble-mat
Spray	Du-ster	Toi-let-roll
Pegs	Light-bulb	Flow-er-pot
Brush	Bo-ttle	
Cup	Dust-pan	
Dish	Tin-foil	

* Place each object at either end of the large space

@learninglady

SYLLABLE SCRAMBLE

How To Play

1. Begin with everyone in the center of the large space.

2. Show the children each of the objects in turn. Can they name each object?

3. Practise clapping the beats or syllables in each word all together. Remember, the syllables are the 'beats' in words, each syllable or beat is created by a vowel.

4. Place each object at opposite ends of the large space. Explain that the children are going to listen out for clapping clues, then run to the object with the matching number of 'beats' or syllables.

5. Demonstrate by clapping the number of syllables in an object, then running to the corresponding object

6. Show the children how to return to the center of the space, ready to play again with the next clapping clue.

7. Encourage the children to listen carefully to the clapping clues, guiding by making choices between 1 and 3 syllables in the beginning.
For example: "Could it be the cup? (1 clap), or the toilet roll? (3 claps)."

8. Play the game several times, speeding up the clapping and running for a real syllable scramble.

9. Make the game more challenging as the children develop in skill and confidence. Increase the number of objects, including similar numbers of syllables (2 and 3 or 3 and 4) to encourage more complex differentiation between beats in words.

Keep Playing!

* Turn this into a rhyming race by calling out a word which rhymes with one of the objects instead of clapping the syllables.

* Turn this into active alliteration by using 2 alliterative items (a colourful cloth and a big bottle), racing to the correct items as they are called. Make this harder by including 2 objects beginning with the same spoken sound (e.g., big bottle and a blue balloon)

* Turn this into an outdoor oral blending game by calling out the separate spoken sounds in the objects (choose simple 3 letter words) for the children to blend the sounds, running to the corresponding object.

ALL ABOARD!

step 3

The children will be preparing for phonics by

* Keeping a steady beat and learning rhymes from memory helps develop an understanding that words are different lengths and made from 'chunks' of spoken sound.

What you need

* Some chairs (or objects to sit on) arranged in a line to create a pretend train.

How To Play

1. Explain that the children are going to be playing a game using the pretend train.
   Line the children up as if they are standing at the station.

2. Begin by saying this rhyme aloud, with the children tapping a steady beat for the motion of the train.

   "Getting on the fast train,
   ready for a ride,
   don't forget your ticket,
   (Add a name) step inside."

3. Act out taking a pretend ticket from the named child, who then gets onto the pretend train.

super sounds

4. Encourage all the children to join in with the following chant, again tapping out a steady beat for the motion of the train.

*"Clackety clack,
Clackety clack,
Clackety clackety
Clackety clack"*

5. Repeat the process of saying both parts of the rhyme all together, maintaining a steady beat.
Choose more children until everyone is seated on the train.

6. Now change the rhyme as the children leave the train, slowing the pace of the rhyme.

*"Coming to the station,
The fast train starts to slow.
Choo choo wave goodbye
(Add a name) off you go."*

7. The named child waves goodbye and leaves the train as the remaining children to join in chanting as before.

*"Clackety clack,
Clackety clack,
Clackety, clackety,
Clackety clack"*

8. Repeat the process with further children until all the 'passengers' are off the train.

9. Encourage as much participation as possible including joining in the rhyme and tapping a steady beat for the motion of the train.

ALL ABOARD!

Watch This Game on YouTube

www.learninglady.co.uk/all-aboard

A great book to read with this game!

The Train Ride by June Crebbin

IN A JAM

step 3

The children will be preparing for phonics by

* Clapping or playing the syllables or beats in words. This helps the children understand that whole words can be broken down into smaller chunks, ready for reading and spelling later.

What you need

* A range of toy vehicles, the names of these need to contain a varied number of syllables or 'beats'
For example:
Car (1 syllable or clap)
Lo-rry (2 syllables or claps)
Bi-cy-cle (3 syllables or claps)

How To Play

1. Talk to the children about their experiences of being stuck in traffic. Explain that the children are going to be playing a traffic jam game with the toy vehicles.
Begin by chanting.

    "We are in a traffic jam,
    Traffic jam, traffic jam,
    We are in a traffic jam.
    Beep, beep beep."

2. Practise chanting this all together until the children begin to join in.

@learninglady

IN A JAM

3. Show the children the first vehicle from the collection. Can they clap the beats or syllables to match the object?
For example: "tra-ctor" (2 claps)

4. Say the sentence "I can see a trac-tor" all together, clapping the syllables or 'beats' in the vehicle name as it is spoken.
Place this on the floor in front of the children. This is the start of the traffic jam.

5. Then repeat the original chant all together.

> "We are in a traffic jam,
> Traffic jam, traffic jam,
> We are in a traffic jam.
> Beep, beep beep."

6. Introduce a second vehicle. Name then clap the number of beats or syllables to match the object all together.
For example: am-bu-lance (3 claps)

7. Place the second vehicle behind the first to add to the traffic jam, then repeat the sentence all together.
"I can see a tra-ctor (2 claps) and an am-bu-lance (3 claps)"

8. Support the children by pointing to each object in the traffic jam as it is recalled.

9. Continue following this pattern of chanting, clapping, adding to the traffic jam, then recalling, until all the vehicles have been included in the traffic jam.

Watch This Game on YouTube

www.learninglady.co.uk/traffic-jam-game

A great book to read with this game!

Car, Car, Truck, Jeep by Katrina Charman and Nick Sharratt

@learninglady

super sounds

Step 4

Let's learn to break spoken words into chunks by hearing, copying and making rhymes

MAGICAL WORDS

step 4

The children will be preparing for phonics by

* Hearing the similarities and differences in word endings.
* Hearing, joining in with and remembering rhyming patterns.

What you need

* A collection of rhyming objects.
  For example: a bug, a jug, a mug, and a plug
* A magic cloth

How To Play

1. Explain that you are going to be playing a magical game with some rhyming objects.

2. Say the name of each object all together, taking care to over emphasise the rhyming ending of each word.
   For example: b-ug, j-ug, m-ug, pl-ug.

3. Remind the children that these are rhyming objects because the end of these words sounds the same.

4. Explain that the children need to look carefully at the objects as the magic will make something disappear.

5. Say the words 4 times all together in a rhyming string to help the children remember, pointing to each object as you say them.
   For example, "bug, jug, mug, plug, bug, jug, mug, plug".

super sounds

6. Lay the magic cloth over the items and say some magic words.

7. Remove an object by grabbing it inside the cloth.

8. Chant the list of words all together again to work out the missing object. For example, "bug, jug, ..., plug, bug, jug, ... plug".

9. Can the children guess what the missing object might be?

10. When the children have offered their ideas, provide a big reveal so the children can check if they guessed correctly.

11. Chant all the names of the objects in the group one last time to check that the items have been returned, then play again.

12. Remove further objects one at a time.

13. Make the game easier by beginning with just two rhyming objects, increasing the number of objects gradually.

14. Add more challenge by adding more objects to the rhyming collection, or by removing more items each time

Watch This Game on YouTube

@learninglady

MAGICAL WORDS

www.learninglady.co.uk/magical-words

A great book to read with this game!

What's in the Witches Kitchen by Nick Sharratt

BAGS OF FUN

step 4

The children will be preparing for phonics by

* Hearing the similarities and differences in word endings
* Matching rhyming words

What you need

* 2 gift bags, shopping bags, or pillowcases (bag A and bag B)
* 5 rhyming pairs of objects. For example, a dog and a frog, soap and a rope, a shell and a bell, a pig and a wig
* Put one object from each pair in bag A, and one object from each pair in bag B.

How To Play

1. Explain that the children are going to sort out the objects in the bags by finding the objects which rhyme.

2. Show the children each of the objects to check that they can name them.

3. Put the objects from each rhyming pair back into bags A and B, emphasising the rhyme as you do so.

4. Remind the children that two words rhyme when the ending sounds the same.
   For example, d-og and fr-og. Explain that these rhyme because they have the same -og ending.

@learninglady

BAGS OF FUN

5. Begin the game by encouraging the children to take it in turns to take 1 object from bag A, and 1 object from bag B. Encourage all the children to try to work out if this is a rhyming pair by emphasising the ending of the words.

6. If the pair rhymes, these can be removed from the bags and set aside in the middle of the group.

7. If the pair doesn't rhyme, the objects need to be put back into bag A and bag B.

8. Play continues in this way, with the children taking turns to match the items from the bags, until all the pairs have been matched.

9. To end the game, go through all the pairs in the middle of the space. With everybody joining in, say the names of the objects, emphasising the rhymes once more.

💡 TRY THIS

Add a Christmas twist by using Santa's sacks for the rhyming pairs.

Keep on Playing!

* Turn this into an alliteration pairs game, using two sets of the same objects in bags A and B. For example, 2 x blue balloons, 2 x smelly socks, 2 x mini marshmallows, 2 x bubble bath etc.

* Turn this into oral blending pairs game in the same way, using 2 sets of everyday 3 letter (cvc) objects. For example, 2 x t-i-n,tin, 2 x h-a-t, hat, 2 x t-u-b, tub, 2 x m-a-p map etc.

Watch This Game on YouTube

www.learninglady.co.uk/bags-of-fun

A great book to read with this game!

The Cat and the Rat and the Hat by Em Lymas

@learninglady

123

PIRATES RHYMING TREASURE

step 4

The children will be preparing for phonics by

* Hearing the similarities and differences in word endings
* Matching rhyming words
* Listening for words which don't rhyme

What you need

* A treasure chest (you could make this with the children)
* A bin or bin bag
* A collection of objects which follow a rhyming pattern. For example, a clock, a rock, a sock, and a lock.
* A picture of one of the rhyming objects needs to be stuck onto the treasure chest. This could be a photo, a drawing, or an image.
* Stick it on with adhesive putty such as blu tac so that you can play the game with different rhymes each time.
* A collection of further objects which don't follow this rhyming pattern. For example, a bear, a shoe, a hat, a bag, a wig, a spoon, and a bowl.
* Hide all of the objects from both collections around the space. You need plenty of items in total, at least 3 per child.
* Place the treasure chest and the bin in the middle of the space
* A map and a pirate hat as props for the adult, and pirate hats for the children (optional)

How To Play

1. Explain that the children are going to be pirates who hunt for treasure.

2. Explain that Pirate Pete only wants treasure that rhymes with the picture on the front of the chest. Show the children the picture as a clue from Pirate Pete. For example, if a picture of king has been stuck onto the treasure chest, some treasure might include a ring, some string, and a spring.

3. Encourage the children to think of some rhyming treasure items, reminding them that words rhyme when the ending of these words sounds the same.

4. Explain that Pirate Pete has hidden lots of items for the children to find (in the role of pirates), but not everything that Pirate Pete has hidden is treasure. Some of the things will need to go in the bin. These will be the things which don't rhyme with the picture on the front of the treasure chest.

5. Demonstrate by hunting around the area looking for an object. Bring the object back to the children in the middle of the space, showing them how to decide if an object is rhyming treasure, or if it needs to go in the bin.

6. Set the children off hunting for treasure in the role of pirates. They'll need to collect 1 object at a time, returning to the treasure chest and the bin in the middle. Can the children sort the objects into treasure, or by putting them into the bin?

7. The game continues, with the children collecting and sorting the items, until everything has been collected.
   Gather the children to check the treasure chest. Name each of the objects aloud to check that they rhyme.

8. Next, search through the bin. Check the name of each item all together, listening out for the ending in case one of the items has gone into the bin and needs to be moved to the treasure.

CATCH THAT FLY

step 4

The children will be preparing for phonics by

* Hearing the similarities and differences in word endings
* Matching rhyming words

What you need

* A set of simple fly swats
* Sets of rhyming picture pairs; these could be from a commercial game, photos of real rhyming objects, drawn pictures or clip art images. Make sure the children know what all the images are before beginning.
* Adhesive putty (like Blu Tac or similar)
* A large space to play, this could be on a wall, on the floor, or spread across a couple of tables. Spread out the pictures and attach them to the space using the adhesive putty. Make sure the picture pairs are well spread out as the children will be 'swatting' these at the same time.

This is a game best played in pairs to maintain safety.

How To Play

1. Introduce the fly swats as a means of 'catching' a fly. Explain that the children are going to catch a fly by listening out for some rhyming clues.

2. Remind the children that words rhyme when the ending sounds the same.

3. Demonstrate by saying aloud "mat", modelling how to look closely at the pictures to 'swat' a picture which rhymes with mat (this could be a cat or a rat picture).

4. Follow with more examples until the children grasp the concept that they will be 'swatting' pictures which rhyme with the words you're saying aloud.

5. Give each child a fly swatter, building momentum by starting with "bbbzzzzzzz....." then saying aloud a word to match one of the rhyming pictures. The children will need to look for a corresponding rhyming picture to swat as quickly as possible.

6. Continue playing by 'swatting' different pictures, using different rhyming clues each time.

💡 TOP TIP

You could add a timer and keep a score of how many rhyming pictures the children can 'swat' in 1 or 2 minutes.

Watch This Game on YouTube

@learninglady

CATCH THAT FLY

www.learninglady.co.uk/catch-that-fly

A great book to read with this game!

There Was An Old Lady Who Swallowed A Fly by Kate Toms

super sounds

Step 5

Let's learn to hear the similarities and differences in spoken sounds at the start of words

SUPERMARKET SORT

step 5

The children will be preparing for phonics by

* Hearing and saying similarities and differences between spoken sounds at the beginning of words.

What you need

* 4 or more branded bags from different supermarkets
  For example, Asda, Morrison's, Tesco, Sainsbury's
* Everyday shopping items which begin with the same initial sounds as the supermarket bags
  For example, apples (Asda), mushrooms (Morrison's), toothpaste (Tesco), soup (Sainsbury's).
* You'll need up to 6 items to sort for each different supermarket bag used. Place these in a box in the center of the space.

How To Play

1. Explain that the children are going to be supermarket sorters because the supermarket shopping has been delivered and it's in a muddle.

2. Introduce the bags from the different supermarkets, emphasising the initial spoken sounds at the beginning of shop names. For example, M-orrisons, S- ainsburys.

3. Explain that the children will need to listen to the first spoken sounds in the objects, matching these with the corresponding shopping bags with the same initial spoken sound.

super sounds

4. As each child takes an item from the muddled shopping box, encourage the children to name that item all together. Model emphasisng the initial spoken sound with the children joining in.
   For example: "mmmmmmmmelon".

5. Can the children work out which bag the melon will go into?
   For example:

   "Could it be mmmmm melon from SsssssssSainsbury's, mmmmmmmm melon from aaaaaaAsda, mmmmmmmelon from ttttttttTesco or mmmmmmelon from Mmmmmmorrisons?"

6. Depending on the confidence and listening ability of the children, work together or encourage them to have a go at working this out as independently.

7. Continue the process, with the children choosing objects to sort into the corresponding bags until all the shopping is organised. Can the children think of further items to go in each branded bag?

> 💡 **TOP TIP**
>
> Once the children are confident in hearing the initial sound similarities, you can begin to talk together about the written letters on the shopping. This introduces the correspondence between spoken sounds and written letters.

SUPERMARKET SORT

Watch This Game on YouTube

New Phase 1 Alliteration Game
super sounds

www.learninglady.co.uk/supermarket-sort

A great book to read with this game!

Supermarket Zoopermarket by Nick Sharratt

134

super sounds

SIMPLE STORIES

step 5

The children will be preparing for phonics by

* Hearing and saying similarities between spoken sounds at the beginning of words.

What you need

* A collection of items which all begin with the same spoken sound.
  For example:
  B-ubble b-ath, B-lue b-rush, P-ink p-yjamas, B-ig b-rown b-ear, S-nuggly S-lippers, T-asty T-oothpaste
* Put all the objects in an overnight bag or suitcase ready to play.

How To Play

1. Explain that you have some bedtime objects in your overnight bag. The children are going to use these for a bedtime storytelling game.

2. Introduce each of the objects, checking that the children know what they are.

3. Use the allterative phrases to describe the objects. For example, "Pink Pyjamas".

4. Explain that both words begin with the same spoken sound, modelling by exaggerating these as you say the word.
   For example, pppppppink pppppppyjamas.

5. Name each object in this way, encouraging the children to join in all together as they are placed into the bag.

@learninglady

SIMPLE STORIES

6. Begin the simple story by saying aloud: "When I get ready for bed, I need my…"

7. Choose an object from the overnight bag, naming the object aloud as it is placed before the children. "Tasty toothpaste".

8. Encourage the children to repeat the sentence aloud again, all together. "When I get ready for bed, I need tasty toothpaste".

9. Choose a child to complete the next part of the story.

10. Say the whole initial sentence aloud all together, encouraging as much joining in as possible. For example:
"When I get ready for bed, I need my tasty toothpaste and……

11. As the child takes the next item from the bag, they need to use the two word alliterative phrase to complete the sentence, for example "snuggly slippers".

12. Some children struggle to describe the object beyond one word "slippers". You will need to repeat and improve on the sentence by saying, "that's right, you've got the slippers, the sssssssnuggly ssssssslippers. "

13. List the items taken from the bag so far, naming them aloud with the children joining in all together as you point to the objects:
For example, "tasty toothpaste, snuggly slippers."

14. Repeat the process as the next child takes an object from the overnight bag and the story building continues.
"When I get ready for bed I need my tasty toothpaste, snuggly slippers and…… my big brown bear".

15. Continue building up the simple story in this way until the objects have been removed from the overnight bag. Keep modelling and encouraging the children to join in as much as possible, using the real objects to support memory, and vocabulary development, especially as more objects are added to the list.

> 💡 **TOP TIP**
>
> Try recording the children so that they can listen back to their alliterative storytelling or use different contexts like,
> "When I went on holiday, I took…" or "When I went to the supermarket I bought…"

Watch This Game on YouTube

SIMPLE STORIES

www.learninglady.co.uk/simple-stories

A great book to read with this game!

Bathroom Boogie by Clare Foges

COOKIE TIME!

step 5

The children will be preparing for phonics by

* Hearing and saying similar spoken sounds at the beginning of words.

What you need

* A toy (or real) cookie
* Think of alliterative names for each of the children. This could be a descriptive word beginning with the same spoken sound as the name. For example: Super Sam, Clever Kitty, Merry Molly, Funny Phoebe, Jumpy Jack, Smiley Sona, Happy Hamza

How To Play

1. Show the children the cookie and explain that one of the children is going to 'steal' the cookie.

2. The children are going to sing a song to find out who it is.

3. Begin by teaching the children the Cookie Jar song or simply chant without a tune, using the adults as an example:

@learninglady

COOKIE TIME!

Everybody sings together.

♫

"Who stole the cookie from the cookie jar?
Adult sings and picks a child, inserting the alliterative name.
Clever Kitty stole the cookie from the cookie jar.
Chosen child sings with adult help.
Not I stole the cookie from the cookie jar,
Everybody sings together.
Then who stole the cookie from the cookie jar?

4. Practise the song so that the children get an idea of who sings / says which part of the song, encouraging as much joining in as possible.

5. Ask the children to close their eyes while the cookie is hidden. Make sure the children have their hands behind their backs.

6. While the children's eyes are closed, secretly give one of the children the cookie, hiding it in their hands so it can't be seen by any of the other children.

7. Begin singing the song again. As children are chosen, don't forget to use the alliterative version of their names, asking them to show their hands to reveal the cookie, or show that the cookie is not there.

8. Always leave the child with the cookie as last to be chosen.

9. Repeat so that all children get a chance to 'steal' the cookie, encouraging greater participation as the children hear the song / chant repeatedly.

TWIZZLE MY TONGUE

step 5

The children will be preparing for phonics by

* Hearing and saying similar spoken sounds at the beginning of words
* Remembering and recalling a simple word sequence

What you need

* A collection of simple tongue twisters suitable for preschool aged children.
* 3- 4-word phrases are great to start with, here are some you could try:

Sam saw six swans
Cheeky chimps chomp chocolate
Baker Bob bakes biscuits
Scary Snakes slither slowly
Mo munches mini marshmallows
Clever Cleo cleans cars
A happy hippo had hiccups
Five fireworks flash and flicker
Sequins sparkle on silver suits
Ten tigers try terrible tricks

* A microphone (real or homemade)

TWIZZLE MY TONGUE

How To Play

1. Choose one tongue twister to practise saying aloud all together. Practise saying it slowly with increasing speed, encouraging the children to join in as much as possible.

2. Emphasise the same initial sound in the words, for example, "Sssssscary sssssss-snakes ssssss-slither ssssss-slowly".

3. Explain that you are going to say the tongue twister aloud again, however this time one of the words will be missing. The children will fill in the missing word from the tongue twister.
For example
"Scary snakes...... slowly"
Can the children work out and say the missing word aloud?

4. Now add the microphone. Repeat the process, this time by saying some of the words into the microphone, leaving a gap and pointing the microphone towards the children when it's their turn to fill the missing gap.
For example
Adult speaking into the microphone "Scary snakes..."
Point the microphone to the children to fill in the gap "slither."
Adult speaking into the microphone "slowly"

5. Repeat using the microphone, missing out different words from the tongue twister each time.
Adult speaking into the microphone "Scary..."
Point the microphone to the children to fill in the gap "snakes."
Adult speaking into the microphone "slither slowly"

6. As children grow in confidence, memory, and skill, miss out more words or encourage independent articulation of tongue twisters. Repeat with different tongue twisters, with increasing words and speeds

💡 TOP TIP

Be mindful of the speech sound developmental difficulties experienced by some children when selecting the tongue twisters. Also consider the use of visual aids or props if the children struggle with the memory aspect of the game.

Watch This Game on YouTube

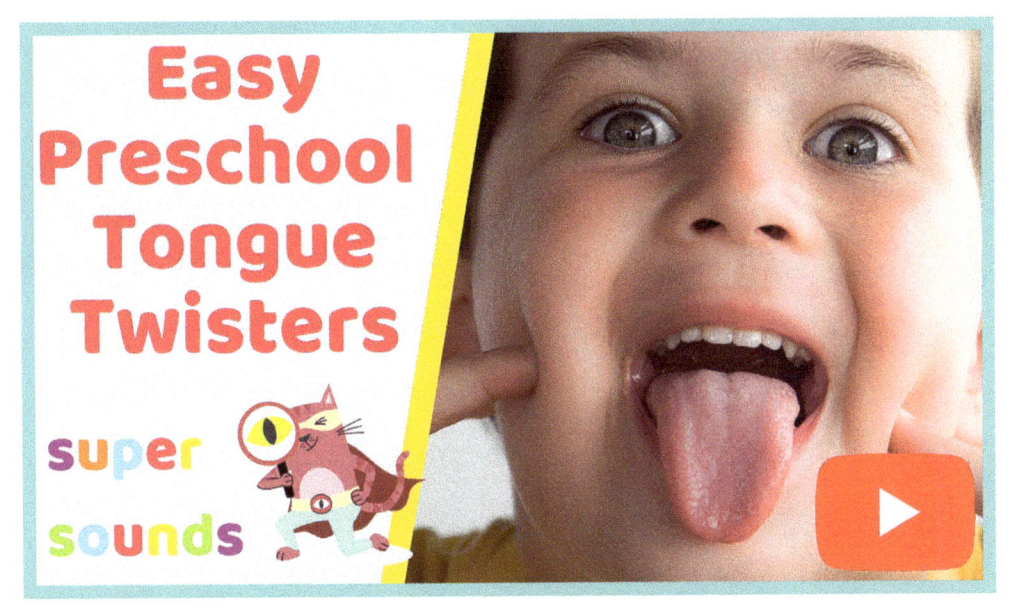

www.learninglady.co.uk/tongue-twisters

TWIZZLE MY TONGUE

A great book to read with this game!

The Wonky Donkey
by Craig Smith

ANIMAL OUTFITS

step 5

The children will be preparing for phonics by

* Hearing and saying similarities in spoken sounds at the beginning of words.

What you need

* 2 foam dice with plastic wallets to add pictures, or cubes with the pictures stuck on. You could also make your own.
* 6 pictures of animals to be added to the dice. These can be drawn or use clip art images.
  For example, a h-ippo, a c-amel, a d-og, a sh-eep, a s-nake, a p-ig
* 6 pictures of types of clothing with an initial sound which matches the animals.
  For example, a h-at, a c-oat, a d-ress, a sh-irt, a s-carf, p-yjamas
* Lots of different dressing up clothes for the children to dress up in. These could match the initial spoken sounds in the children's names.

How To Play

1. Explain that the children are going to be playing a dressing up game by listening out for words which have the same spoken sound at the beginning.

2. Demonstrate by saying pairs like "H-ippo, H-at, C-ardigan, C-at, C-amel, C-oat, "emphasisng the initial sounds in these words. Practise saying these all together.

@learninglady

145

ANIMAL OUTFITS

3. The children will take it in turns to roll both dice at the same time. The aim of the game is to roll 2 objects which begin with the same spoken sound. For example, h-ippo and h-at.

4. If a child rolls two pictures which do begin with the same spoken sound, they can choose, and wear, an item of fun clothing from the collection. This could match the initial spoken sounds in their name if you're playing with more confident children.

5. If a child rolls two pictures which don't begin with the same spoken sound, they must pass the dice onto the next player, without dressing up.

6. Play in this way, rolling, matching, and passing the dice, and dressing up until all the clothes are being worn by the children.

7. Take some funky photos of the fun outfits that the children have created.

💡 TOP TIP

It helps to over-emphasise the initial spoken sounds in words, pointing out when these are the same and when these are different.

Watch This Game on YouTube

super sounds

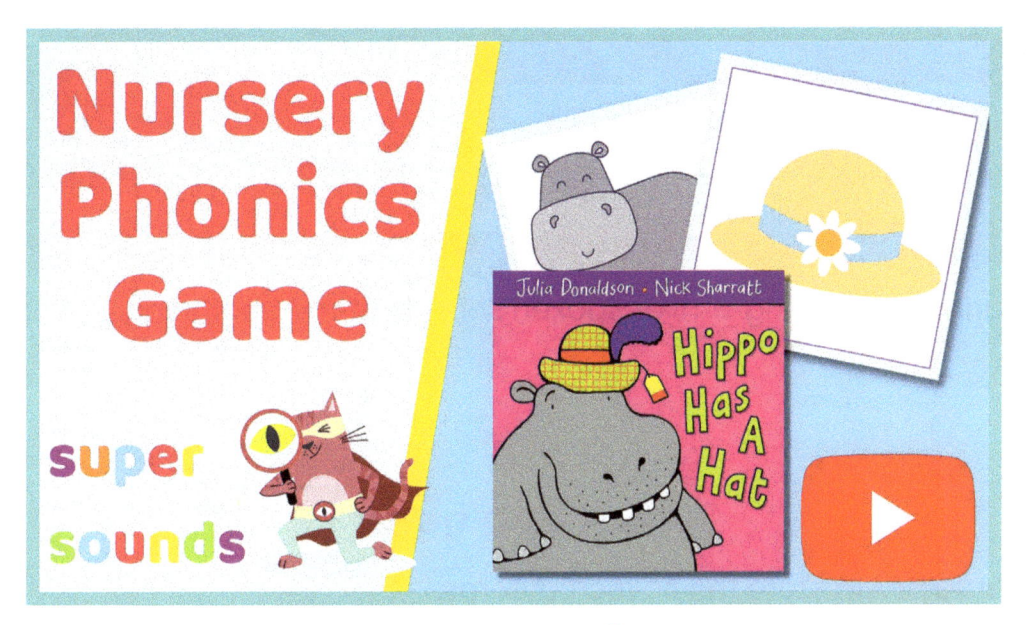

www.learninglady.co.uk/animal-outfits

A great book to read with this game!

Hippo Has a Hat by Julia Donaldson and Nick Sharratt

SEARCHING FOR STUFF — step 5

The children will be preparing for phonics by
* Hearing and saying similar spoken sounds at the beginning of words.

What you need
* A large box to store the collected items.
* Collect, or think of, everyday household or classroom objects which can be hidden. These need to incorporate alliterative patterns, when two words next to each other begin with the same spoken sound. Write these down in a list. **For example:**
  A pink pencil, snipping scissors, purple paper, Christmas card, sparkling sequins, big block, sticky sellotape, bouncy ball, bean bag, hula hoop, pig puppet, squirty soap. You'll need to think of no less that 3 objects per player.
* A 5-minute timer (you could use any device for this)

How To Play

1. Introduce the large box and the list, explaining that the children need to find all the objects from your list, filling the box as quickly as possible.

2. Using the alliterative patterns previously written in the list, assign each child with an object to find.
   For example
   "Hamza, can you find me a purple pen, Lily can you find me some red ribbon, and Kai can you find me a shiny shell."

3. This is a timed game, so the children need to find the objects as quickly as possible. Remind the children that the aim of the game is for the children to collect all the items on the list, filling the box before the 5-minute timer sounds.

4. Check that the children know what they are looking for, reminding them to use both alliterative words to describe each item.
For example
"I'm looking for a purple pen".

5. Remodel both alliterative words if the children are still at the one-word naming stage.

6. Set the timer and observe the children as they search for the alliterative items, supporting as necessary.

7. As children find the items and return to the box, check again to see if they can use the alliterative words to describe what they've collected. Check each found item off the list together, providing each child with a new alliterative object to find.

8. Continue issuing new words, as the children search, find, then check off alliterative items, until either the timer sounds, or all the objects are collected from the list.

9. At the end of the game, gather the children to check the contents of the box.

10. Using the list, read each of the alliterative items aloud. Can the children match the spoken words with the objects in the box?

super sounds

Step 6

Let's learn to hear to hear and say separate sounds in words, ready for making and reading words when school starts

I HEAR WITH MY LITTLE EAR

step 6

The children will be preparing for phonics by

* Orally blending phonemes (spoken sounds) segmented by an adult
* Practising orally segmenting (breaking down spoken sounds) following an adult model

What you need

* A story with detailed and interesting pictures with lots of things to spot. For example, Stick Man, The Snail and the Whale or The Smartest Giant in Town, all by Julia Donaldson and Axel Scheffler

How To Play

1. This game is like a classic game of I Spy. In this game though, the emphasis doesn't focus on the first spoken sound in words.

2. The objective is to hear, then blend, all the separate spoken sounds in words, matching these with an object.

3. Begin by looking at the book together. Talk about the pictures, relating these to what the children already know.

4. Start the game by saying:
   "I hear with my little ear, something that sounds like…. d-o-g"

5. Say each of the separate sounds in the word, beginning with a simple 3 letter (cvc) word in the picture.

super sounds

6. Support the children by blending the sounds together, then matching the blended word with the corresponding object.

7. Follow this process with several items in each picture.

8. Remind the children to look closely at the illustrations as they listen to the spoken sounds in the chosen word.

9. If the children are confident, let them have a go at offering the clues by orally segmenting themselves.

> 💡 **TOP TIP**
>
> To challenge more confident oral blenders and segmenters, use longer words matched to objects in illustrations, (these are often known as cvcc, consonant-vowel-consonant-consonant or ccvc words)
> For example, l-a-m-p, b-e-l-t, f-r-o-g, p-a-rr-o-t

Watch This Game on YouTube

@learninglady

I HEAR WITH MY LITTLE EAR

www.learninglady.co.uk/I-hear-with-my-little-ear

A great book to read with this game!

Monkey Puzzle
by Julia Donaldson

WHAT'S THE WORD MR. WOLF?

step 6

The children will be preparing for phonics by

* Orally segmenting; hearing and saying all the separate spoken sounds in words.

What you need

* This is best played in large space- outdoors is ideal.
* Before beginning, make a list of words you're going to be using. Words which include 3 separate spoken sounds (often known as c-v-c or consonant-vowel-consonant words) are best to start with. These could include words like:
c-a-t, f-o-x, h-e-n, p-o-t, l-i-p, c-a-n

How To Play

1. Explain that you are going to be Mr. Wolf and you are going to try to catch the children.

2. Organise the space so that you are standing at one end of the space as 'Mr Wolf', with the children standing at the opposite end of the space. This should look like a traditional game of 'What's the time Mr Wolf?' It might be helpful to enlist the help of a second adult to join in with the children when they are learning how to play.

3. Teach the children to begin by chanting the phrase "What's the word Mr Wolf?'

4. In the role of Mr Wolf, say aloud one of your preprepared whole words. **For example,** "lip"

WHAT'S THE WORD MR. WOLF?

5. The children will need to think about the number of phonemes (spoken sounds) they can hear in the word, then take the corresponding number of steps towards Mr Wolf, orally segmenting out loud as they do so.
For example, "l-i-p" (3 steps, one for each separate spoken sound). The children should say each separate phoneme (spoken sound) as they step.

6. Play continues in this way, with the children chanting, "What's the word Mr. Wolf," Mr. Wolf calling out a whole word, then the children saying and stepping out the correct number of phonemes (spoken sounds) in each word.

7. As play continues, the children will be stepping nearer and nearer to Mr. Wolf.

8. When the children have almost reached Mr. Wolf, and have chanted 'What's the word Mr. Wolf?
Mr. Wolf shouts out '"Dinnertime"!

9. The children should run as quickly as they can back to the starting point where they are safe and ready to play again.

10. Mr. Wolf must try to 'catch' one of the children. They can then become the new Mr. Wolf as the game begins again.

11. Repeat as many times as possible so the children get plenty of practise.

Watch This Game on YouTube

www.learninglady.co.uk/whats-the-word

WHAT IS IT?

step 6

The children will be preparing for phonics by
* Orally segmenting spoken sounds matched to real objects
* Orally blending spoken sounds matched to real objects

What you need
* A collection of real objects. These should be objects which include 3 separate spoken sounds (often known as c-v-c or consonant-vowel-consonant words). You need 1 object for each child playing.
* A box big enough to hold all the objects. Put the objects inside the box before beginning.

How To Play

1. Explain that the children will be singing a song then guessing one of the mystery objects inside a mystery box. The children will take turns to look inside the box, giving sound clues for their friends to guess what's inside.

2. Show the children each of the objects as you put them into the box, checking that they know what each object is. Orally segment each object together as it is placed into the box.

3. Sing the 'Something's hiding' song, encouraging everyone to join in all together:

super sounds

"Something's hiding in the box,
In the box, in the box,
Something's hiding in the box,
Let's find out what's inside."

Sing to the tune of Here We Go Round the Mulberry Bush

Sing along with instant streaming!

4. As the singing ends, choose one of the children to look inside the box. Explain that they need to look at the objects inside, without telling anyone what is there.

5. This child then gives a clue about the chosen object, by segmenting the object into its separate spoken sounds.
For example, if the chosen object is a cat, the child will say c-a-t. as a clue.

6. The other children work out what the object is by orally blending the spoken sounds together.

7. The child offering the clue should reveal the object which is then removed from the box.

8. Everyone continues by singing the second verse of the song all together.

WHAT IS IT?

♪

"(Add name) picked a c-a-t,
c-a-t, c-a-t,
(Add name) picked a c-a-t
That's what was inside."

Sing to the tune of Here We Go Round the Mulberry Bush

9. Continue the process with different children giving the clues until all the children have had a turn and there are no more objects in the box.

Watch This Game on YouTube

www.learninglady.co.uk/what-is-it

PIRATES WALK THE PLANK

step 6

The children will be preparing for phonics by

* Orally blending phonemes (spoken sounds) segmented by an adult
* Remembering and matching orally blended words to real objects

What you need

* A plank of wood placed in the middle of the space
* A treasure chest (this could be made by the children). Place this at the end of the plank
* A collection of objects or 'treasure". Ideally these should be objects which include 3 separate spoken sounds (often known as c-v-c or consonant-vowel-consonant words). You could include words like d-o-g, b-a-t, p-e-n, l-i-d, m-u-g, t-i-n, m-a-n. These need to be stored in the treasure chest at the beginning of the game
* Pirate hats for the adults and children (optional)
* Parrot puppet or toy

How To Play

1. Explain that the Pirate Captain has a cheeky parrot who is going to give the pirate children some clues to steal some of the Pirate Captain's treasure. The children (in the role of pirates) will need to listen carefully to the clues, creeping down the plank to grab the matching items from the treasure chest, returning to safety by creeping back up the plank with each object.

2. The children (in the role of pirates) will need to work out what this object is by orally blending the spoken sounds together.
   For example,
   Using the parrot puppet in role, "Can you steal a ....p-e-n."

@learninglady

PIRATES WALK THE PLANK

3. Choose one of the pirate children to creep down the plank to find the matching object from the chest, returning up the plank to the safety, without making a sound to wake up the Pirate Captain.

4. Once all the treasure has been 'stolen' from the chest, practise even more oral blending as the parrot checks the items.

5. As the parrot orally segments some of the objects "m-u-g", can the children orally blend and match objects by standing up when their items are segmented by the parrot?

💡 TOP TIP

Make sure you say the spoken sounds in the purest way possible as this is the method used when children begin more formal Phonics teaching later. The Alphablocks TV show provides adults and children with a great example of how to say the spoken sounds correctly, this can be found easily online.

A great book to read with this game!

Portside Pirates
by Laura Andrews

SUPER SOUNDS DISCO

step 6

The children will be preparing for phonics by

* Orally blending phonemes (spoken sounds) segmented by an adult
* Remembering and matching orally blended words to real objects

What you need

* A large space to dance around in
* Favourite dance music a device to play the music on
* A collection of objects. These should be objects which include 3 separate spoken sounds (often known as c-v-c or consonant-vowel-consonant words). You could include objects such as a d-o-g, b-a-t, p-e-n, l-i-d, m-u-g, t-i-n, m-a-n. You will need at least 1 object per child playing plus some extras. Spread these around the floor so that the children have plenty of space to move between the objects.
* A large box to tidy the objects into

How To Play

1. Explain that the children are going to play a musical game which begins with them dancing around the space without touching the any of the objects. The children should not move or touch the objects while they are dancing.

2. When the music stops, the children each need to grab an object, standing as still as they can. This part of the game is like a classic game of Musical Statues or Musical Chairs, the children will be simply 'freezing' as they collect an object.

3. When the music stops and the children have all grabbed an object, orally segment (say the separate spoken sounds) for one of the objects. For example, "The object out this time is a ... (d-o-g)"

@learninglady

SUPER SOUNDS DISCO

4. The children will need to orally blend the spoken sounds (phonemes) to work out the object named by the adult.

5. The child holding the segmented object (in this case, the dog) must place the object into the large box as this object (not the child) is out of the game.

6. The children can then replace the remaining objects back onto the floor as the game begins again.

7. Play continues in this way, with further objects placed in the box every time the music is stopped until none of the objects are left on the floor.

A great book to read with this game!

Kitchen Disco by Clare Foges

FINISH IT OFF!

step 6

The children will be preparing for phonics by

* Orally blending the spoken sounds segmented by an adult

What you need

* A well-known picture story book with interesting pictures and a rhyming or rhythmic pattern
  For example, Super Duck by Jez Alborough

How To Play

1. Read the story together a few times before playing. Practise leaving out the rhyming gaps for the children to complete all together. This builds confidence and an awareness of the words you'll be using.

2. Explain that the children are going to help you to read the book.

3. You're going to be giving the children clues by segmenting words (saying the separate sounds). They will need to listen then blend those sounds back together to say the missing words.

4. Try working out some of the selected words in isolation first.
   For example,
   Adult "d-u-ck", Children "duck"
   Adult "g-oa-t, Children "goat"
   Adult "sh-e-d" Children "shed."
   Adult "f-r-o-g" Children "frog"

FINISH IT OFF!

5. Begin by reading the story, then orally segment one word on each page. Picking words at the ends of sentences is ideal to begin with.

6. Encourage the children to join in with orally blending the words aloud by joining in all together. Support the children as required.

7. This activity really builds confidence and the feeling that the children are really reading the book themselves.

A great book to read with this game!

Super Duck by Jez Alborough

DON'T FORGET!

super sounds
The VERY BEST Phonics Programme for Preschool and Nursery children

FREE BONUS BOOKLET

- Simple Assessment Checklist
- Fun Interactive Booklist
- Easy to use Song Book
- Fast resourcing ideas

Download Now!

The Learning Lady

Download your **FREE Super Sounds Bonus Booklet** Now at
www.learninglady.co.uk/super-sounds-bonus-booklet

@learninglady

Super Sounds

Part 2

Super Sounds Super Plans!

super sounds

Get Started with Super Sounds

A year full of listening, attention, and early phonological awareness planning. Systematic stories, songs, games and play ideas for 2-year olds.

★ Getting Started with Super Sounds
Stories songs and rhymes to play with 2-year olds

Finger plays and nursery rhymes and songs to learn with 2-year-olds Learn and play together, Repeat the same ones until toddlers know these off by heart.	**Setting up for learning sounds** Describe the sounds aloud as a model while you play
- Open shut them - This little piggie - Round and round the garden - Pat a cake - Twinkle Twinkle - Incy Wincy - Humpty Dumpty - Baa baa black sheep - Hickory Dickory Dock - This is the way we wash our hands. - I hear thunder - Row row row your boat - If you're happy and you know it - Ring a ring o roses - The farmers in the den - Old Macdonald had a farm	- Go on a learning walk, what do you hear? - Make loud and quiet sounds by trying in different shoes to stomp in together. - Create your own kitchen band, exploring sounds by banging with different kitchen tools. - Make your own shakers by adding rice, pasta, or coins to food containers. - Play hide and seek with a mobile phone by hiding it then ringing it. - Play hide and seek with favourite toys using loud and quiet clapping clues to find them. - Noisy Dice Game (using farm animals, jungle animals, vehicles) - Traffic lights game - Noisy eggs

Playing with sounds Read and play with these on repeat!	Learning intentions We are learning to….
Books - Exploring noisy books. - Exploring lift the flap books. - Exploring touch and feel books. - Reading first word books together - Reading early look and find books together. - Read Character books like: - Maisy by Lucy Cousins - Spot the dog by Eric Hill - Wibbly pig by Mick Inkpen **Playing together** - Modelling sounds matched to objects like trains in a train set, dinosaurs roaring or farm animal toys - Bubble blowing and drinking using a straw. - Shape sorters - Inset puzzles - 2-piece puzzles - Matching socks, shoes, gloves - Matching pairs games - Exploring musical instruments	- Listen and join in with stories, songs, and rhymes. - Make sounds as I join in with stories and songs. - Match the sounds that I've heard with a picture. - Copy the sounds I've heard. - Name some animals / objects and make their sounds.

For quick song links: https://learninglady.co.uk/more-songs-and-rhymes

super sounds

Super Sounds From the Start

**The whole of Super Sounds in a year!
The perfect progression of stories, songs, games, and play ideas for 3- and 4-year-olds**

A Year full of Super Sounds – Daily Pre-phonics with 3- and 4-Year Olds
Term / Semester 1 – Step 1

	Large Group Activities Read the story of the week **EVERYDAY** with increasing participation Sing the song of the week **EVERYDAY** with increasing participation	Small group activities Deliver in a quiet space, free from visual and noise distraction. Play several times throughout the week. Keep group size no larger than 6	Play Provision Enhancements	Optional Take Home Task in: Super Sounds at Home	Learning Intentions We are learning to...
WEEK 1	*Noisy Farm* by Rod Campbell ♪ *Humpty Dumpty*	Noisy Dice Game (using farm animals)	Collection of noisy / sound making books	Noisy Farm	Listen and join in with stories, songs, and games
WEEK 2	*Dear Zoo* by Rod Campbell ♪ *Wind the bobbin up*	Noisy Dice Game (using jungle animals)	Props to go with stories and songs	Noisy Farm	Make sounds as I join in with stories and songs
WEEK 3	*Walking Through the Jungle* ♪ *Incy Wincy Spider*	Pass the Box (using zoo animals)	Add objects to role play e.g., a packet of cereal to shake, an alarm clock, different materials to make sounds with e.g., metal spoons and wooden spoons to stir with	Down in the Jungle	Match the sounds that I've heard with a picture
WEEK 4	*Car, Car, Truck, Jeep* by Nick Sharratt ♪ *The wheels on the bus*	Pass the Box (using vehicles)		Beep, Beep!	Copy the sounds I've heard
WEEK 5	*Farmer Duck* by Martin Waddell ♪ *Old Macdonald had a farm*	Musical Sounds (using farm animals)	Bubble blowing and painting for developing mouth control	Driving My Tractor	Name some animals / objects and make their sounds
WEEK 6	*The Shopping List* by John Burningham ♪ *1,2,3,4,5 once I caught a fish alive*	Listen to the shopping game	Shape sorters and Inset puzzles 2-piece puzzles	Sounds Around!	

super sounds

★ A Year full of Super Sounds – Daily Pre-phonics with 3- and 4-Year Olds
Term / Semester 2 – Step 2

	Large Group Activities Read the story of the week **EVERYDAY** with increasing participation Sing the song of the week **EVERYDAY** with increasing participation	Small group activities Deliver in a quiet space, free from visual and noise distraction. Play several times throughout the week. Keep group size no larger than 6	Play Provision Enhancements	Optional Take Home Task in: Super Sounds at Home	Learning Intentions We are learning to…
WEEK 1	*I want to be a duck* by Oxford Children's Books ♫ *The Drummers in the Ring* – Loud and quiet	Noisy Dice game (with firework symbols)	Musical instrument exploration	Quack, Quack!	Listen and join in with stories, songs, and games
WEEK 2	*A busy day for birds* by Lucy Cousins ♫ *The Drummers in the Ring* – Fast and Slow	Super Sound sequences (using bird pictures, animal pictures or instruments)	Junk model sound maker resources	Busy Birds	Take turns to explore different musical instruments
WEEK 3	*Brown Bear, Brown Bear, What do You See?* by Eric Carle and Bill Martin Jr ♫ *Pass the Tambourine*	Copy my claps game (using the animals from the story)	Props to go with stories and songs	What can you see?	Play instruments to make different sorts of sounds e.g., fast / slow / loud / quiet
WEEK 4	*Dinosaur Roar* by Paul Strickland ♫ *Feel the beat*	Musical hide and seek game (using a toy dinosaur)	Blowing light objects (feathers, pom poms, sequins) with straws to increase control of air through the lips	Dinosaur Roar!	Match the way I play an instrument with a symbol or instruction
WEEK 5	*The Dinky Donkey* by Craig Smith ♫ *A sailor went to sea, sea, sea*	Twizzle my tongue	Spot the difference / look and find books in the reading area	Rumbling Dinosaurs	I can name some instruments
WEEK 6	*The Bathroom Boogie* by Clare Foges ♫ *The bear went over the mountain*	Simple Stories: Getting Ready for Bed version	4–6-piece puzzles	Noisy Aliens	Clap a steady beat as I join in with musical activities

177

★ A Year full of Super Sounds – Daily Pre-phonics with 3- and 4-Year Olds
Term / Semester 3 – Step 3

	Large Group Activities Read the story of the week **EVERYDAY** with increasing participation Sing the song of the week **EVERYDAY** with increasing participation	**Small group activities** Deliver in a quiet space, free from visual and noise distraction. Play several times throughout the week. Keep group size no larger than 6	**Play Provision Enhancements**	**Optional Take Home Task in: Super Sounds at Home**	**Learning Intentions** We are learning to....
WEEK 1	We're going on a Bear Hunt by Michael Rosen and Helen Oxenbury ♪ Little Drummers Drumming	Which Animal is Hiding	Musical instrument exploration, including resources used in Term 2	Bear Hunt	Learn simple songs and sing from memory
WEEK 2	The Bus Is for Us by Michael Rosen ♪ Down at the station	In A Jam	A collection of rhythm and rhyme books and matching props / puppets	Get on the bus!	Join in with repeated refrains in stories
WEEK 3	The Train Ride by June Crebbin ♪ Row, row, row your boat	All Aboard!	Real life rhyming objects in the role play home e.g., a mat, a tin and a bin, a jug, and a mug	Train Ride	Copy a rhythm by clapping or using an instrument Repeat a rhythm by clapping or using an instrument
WEEK 4	Pants by Giles Andrea and Nick Sharratt ♪ Pass the Tambourine	Noisy Dice game (with pictures of different pants from the story, clapping the syllables as you roll)	Independent use of resources introduced during focussed activities	Pants!	Make up our own rhythmic patterns
WEEK 5	Kitchen Disco by Clare Foges ♪ The Grand Old Duke of York	Syllable Scramble (Using kitchen items or food)		Have a kitchen disco!	Clap the syllables in our names Clap the syllables in everyday words.
WEEK 6	Veg Patch Party by Clare Foges ♪ If you're happy and you know it	Copy my claps (using vegetables from the story)	8–12-piece puzzles	Veg Patch Party!	Count the syllables in words to sort objects

178

super sounds

★ A Year full of Super Sounds – Daily Pre-phonics with 3- and 4-Year Olds
Term / Semester 4 – Step 4

	Large Group Activities Read the story of the week **EVERYDAY** with increasing participation Sing the song of the week **EVERYDAY** with increasing participation	Small group activities Deliver in a quiet space, free from visual and noise distraction. Play several times throughout the week. Keep group size no larger than 6	Play Provision Enhancements	Optional Take Home Task in: Super Sounds at Home	Learning Intentions We are learning to….
WEEK 1	*The Cat and the Rat and the Hat* by Em Lymas	Noisy Dice Game (with rhyming pictures)		The Cat and the Rat	Join in with rhyming stories and songs
WEEK 2	*Oi Frog!* ♪ *Five little specked frogs*	Magical Words Game	A collection of rhythm and rhyme books and matching props / puppets	Rhyming I Spy	Fill in the rhyming gaps in stories
WEEK 3	*Chocolate Mousse for Greedy Goose* by Julia Donaldson and Nick Sharratt ♪ *We're marching in our wellingtons*	Magical Words Game with different rhyming objects	Real life rhyming objects in the role play home e.g., a cat and a mat, a tin and a bin, a jug and a mug	Yum Yum!	Match rhyming objects from small sets of 6 objects Continue a rhyming string using props / picture
WEEK 4	*Shark in the Park* by Nick Sharratt ♪ *Down in the jungle*	Bags of Fun game	Independent use of resources introduced during focussed activities	Shark in the park	Identify objects in a set which don't rhyme
WEEK 5	*Super Duck* by Jez Alborough ♪ *We're driving in our car*	Bags of Fun game with different rhyming objects	Large floor puzzles	Super Ducks!	Say a rhyming list from memory
WEEK 6	*Row, Row Pirate Boat* ♪ *I'm a pirate*	Pass the box game with rhyming clues		Rhyming with pirates	Makes up our own rhymes

@learninglady

179

★ A Year full of Super Sounds – Daily Pre-phonics with 3- and 4-Year Olds
Term / Semester 5 – Step 5

	Large Group Activities Read the story of the week **EVERYDAY** with increasing participation Sing the song of the week **EVERYDAY** with increasing participation	Small group activities Deliver in a quiet space, free from visual and noise distraction. Play several times throughout the week. Keep group size no larger than 6	Play Provision Enhancements	Optional Take Home Task in: Super Sounds at Home	Learning Intentions We are learning to….
WEEK 1	*Hippo has a Hat* ♪ *This is the way we lay the bricks*	Animal Outfits	Magnetic letters to explore with name cards (capital and lower case)	Dressing Up!	Hear the similarities in the first spoken sounds in words
WEEK 2	*The Wonky Donkey* by Craig Smith ♪ *The wheels on the bus*	Twizzle my tongue	Real life packaging in the role play home e.g., packets, tins, magazines, to draw awareness. Sometimes include alliterative items e.g., a prickly pineapple, straight spaghetti, snuggly slippers	Let's listen	Say the first spoken sounds in words
WEEK 3	*The Dinky Donkey* by Craig Smith ♪ *A sailor went to sea, sea, sea*	The Magical Words game with alliterative items		Spot the Difference	Find two objects beginning with the same sound from a set of objects
WEEK 4	*The Bathroom Boogie* by Clare Foges ♪ *The bear went over the mountain*	Simple Stories: Getting Ready for Bed version		Bathroom Boogie	Sort objects which don't begin with the same spoken sound as others
WEEK 5	*Hooray for fish* by Lucy Cousins ♪ *Heads, shoulders, knees and toes*	The Magical Words game with different alliterative items	Independent use of resources introduced during focussed activities	Let's look	Say a 4-word tongue twister from memory
WEEK 6	*Pete the cat and the perfect pizza party* by James Dean ♪ *Here we go round the mulberry bush*	Simple Stories: I went to the supermarket, and I bought… version	16-piece puzzles	Perfect Pizza	Sort similarities and differences in letter shapes

180

super sounds

A Year full of Super Sounds – Daily Pre-phonics with 3- and 4-Year Olds
Term / Semester 6 – Step 6

	Large Group Activities Read the story of the week **EVERYDAY** with increasing participation Sing the song of the week **EVERYDAY** with increasing participation	Small group activities Deliver in a quiet space, free from visual and noise distraction. Play several times throughout the week. Keep group size no larger than 6	Play Provision Enhancements	Optional Take Home Task in: Super Sounds at Home	Learning Intentions We are learning to...
WEEK 1	*Monkey Puzzle* by Julia Donaldson ♪ *1 finger 1 thumb keep moving*	I Hear with My Little Ear game		I hear with my little ear	Hear all the separate sounds in a spoken cvc word
WEEK 2	*A Squash and a Squeeze* by Julia Donaldson ♪ *Ten in the bed*	What is it game		Which is it?	Say all the spoken sounds in a cvc word
WEEK 3	*The koala who could* by Rachel Bright ♪ ?	The pirate captain says... Oral blending version	Everyday CVC objects in the role play home e.g., cup, bag, hat, rug, cap, pop	Can you hear it?	Orally blend spoken sounds to say the full cvc word
WEEK 4	*The squirrels who squabbled* by Rachel Bright ♪ ?	Noisy dice game (oral blending version)	Independent use of resources introduced during focussed activities	What's my word?	Match orally blended words to corresponding objects / actions
WEEK 5	*Mrs Blackhat* by Mick and Chloe Inkpen ♪ *Hokey Cokey*	Pass the box game (oral blending version)		Let's do magic!	Orally segment words to say each spoken sound separately
WEEK 6	*Mrs Blackhat and the Zoom Broom* by Mick and Chloe Inkpen ♪ *One man went to mow*	What's the word Mr. Wolf		Flying high!	Retell a simple familiar story from memory

@learninglady

181

super sounds

Super Serious about Super Sounds

45-minute teaching sequences following the Super Sounds Success Map

Super Serious about Super Sounds | A Year of Super Sounds Weekly 45-minute sessions
Term / Semester 1a – Step 1

	5 mins	5 mins	5 mins	5 mins	5 mins	5 mins	5 mins	5 mins	Take Home Task
	GAME 1	GAME 2	GAME 3	SONG	JOINING IN STORY	GAME 5	GAME 6	GAME 7	SUPER SOUNDS AT HOME
WEEK 1	The Drummer's in the ring *Loud and quiet*	Choose a sound song	Traffic lights game	*Old Macdonald had a farm*	*Noisy Farm* by Rod Campbell	Pass the box	Noisy Dice Game	Musical sounds	Noisy Farm
WEEK 2	The Drummer's in the ring *Loud and quiet*	Choose a sound song	Traffic lights game	*Old Macdonald had a zoo*	*Dear Zoo* by Rod Campbell	Pass the box	Noisy Dice Game	Musical sounds	Dear Zoo
WEEK 3	The Drummer's in the ring *Loud and quiet*	Choose a sound song	Traffic lights game	*Old Macdonald had a zoo*	*Walking through the jungle* by Julie Lacome	Pass the box	Noisy Dice Game	Musical sounds	Down in the Jungle
WEEK 4	The Drummer's in the ring *Loud and quiet*	Choose a sound song	Traffic lights game	*The wheels on the bus*	*Car, Car, Truck, Jeep* by Katrina Charman and Nick Sharratt	Pass the box	Noisy Dice Game	Musical sounds	Beep, Beep!
WEEK 5	The Drummer's in the ring *Fast and slow*	Choose a sound song	Traffic lights game	*The wheels on the bus*	*Driving my tractor* by Jan Dobbins	Listen to the shopping game	Noisy Eggs	Musical sounds	Driving My Tractor
WEEK 6	The Drummer's in the ring *Fast and slow*	Choose a sound song	Traffic lights game	*Wind the bobbin up*	*Peace at last* by Jill Murphy	Listen to the shopping game	Noisy Eggs	Musical sounds	Sounds Around!
WEEK 7	The Drummer's in the ring *Fast and slow*	Choose a sound song	Traffic lights game	*Wind the bobbin up*	*The Shopping List* by John Burningham	Listen to the shopping game	Noisy Eggs	Musical sounds	Noisy Shopping

The children will be learning to:
- Join in with, match, and copy the everyday sounds I've heard.
- Use some instruments to make different sorts of sounds.
- Join in with action songs and rhymes.
- Name some animals / objects and make their sounds, without seeing them.
- Name different instruments and change how I play them by following instructions e.g fast / slow / loud / quiet.
- Join in with stories and songs, using my mouth to make lots of different sounds and noises.

★ Super Serious about Super Sounds | A Year of Super Sounds Weekly 45-minute sessions
Term / Semester 1b – Step 2

	5 mins	5 mins	5 mins	5 mins	5 mins	5 mins	5 mins	5 mins	Take Home Task
	GAME 1	**GAME 2**	**GAME 3**	**SONG**	**JOINING IN STORY**	**GAME 5**	**GAME 6**	**GAME 7**	**SUPER SOUNDS AT HOME**
WEEK 1	Pass the tambourine around	Feel the beat	Copy my claps	*Down at the station*	*I want to be a duck* by Oxford Children's books	Waddle like a penguin	Super Sound Sequences	The Pirate captain says...	Quack, Quack!
WEEK 2	Pass the tambourine around	Feel the beat	Copy my claps	*Down at the station*	*A busy day for birds* by Lucy Cousins	Waddle like a penguin	Super Sound Sequences	The Pirate captain says...	Busy Birds
WEEK 3	Pass the tambourine around	Feel the beat	Copy my claps	*Down at the station*	*Brown bear, Brown bear what do you see?* by Eric Carle and Bill Martin Junior	Waddle like a penguin	Super Sound Sequences	The Pirate captain says...	What can you see?
WEEK 4	Pass the tambourine around	Feel the beat	Copy my claps	*Incy Wincy Spider*	*Dinosaur roar* by Paul Strickland	Noisy Dice Game	Musical hide and seek	The Pirate captain says...	Dinosaur Roar!
WEEK 5	Pass the tambourine around	Feel the beat	Copy my claps	*Incy Wincy Spider*	*Rumble Rumble Dinosaur* by Katrina chapman	Noisy Dice Game	Musical hide and seek	The Pirate captain says...	Rumbling Dinosaurs
WEEK 6	Pass the tambourine around	Feel the beat	Copy my claps	*Hokey Cokey*	*There's an alien in your book* by Tom Fletcher	Noisy Dice Game	Musical hide and seek	The Pirate captain says...	Noisy Aliens
WEEK 7	Pass the tambourine around	Feel the beat	Copy my claps	*Hokey Cokey*	*I say ooh, you say Ahh* by John Kaner	Noisy Dice Game	Musical hide and seek	The Pirate captain says...	I Say OOH

The children will be learning to:
- Listen and join in with stories, songs, and games.
- Take turns to explore different musical instruments.
- Play instruments to make different sorts of sounds e.g. fast /slow/ loud/quiet.
- Play instruments matched with a symbol or instruction.
- Name some instruments.
- Clap a steady beat as I join in with musical activities.

Super Serious about Super Sounds | A Year of Super Sounds Weekly 45-minute sessions
Term / Semester 2a – Step 3

	5 mins	5 mins	5 mins	5 mins	5 mins	5 mins	5 mins	5 mins	Take Home Task
	GAME 1	GAME 2	GAME 3	SONG	JOINING IN STORY	GAME 5	GAME 6	GAME 7	SUPER SOUNDS AT HOME
WEEK 1	Little drummer's drumming	Choose a sound song	Super Sound Sequences	The Grand Old Duke of York	We're going on a bear hunt by Michael Rosen	Which animal is hiding?	Copy my claps	All Aboard!	Bear Hunt
WEEK 2	Little drummer's drumming	Choose a sound song	Super Sound Sequences	The Grand Old Duke of York	The bus is for us by Michael Rosen	Which animal is hiding?	Copy my claps	All Aboard!	Get on the bus!
WEEK 3	Little drummer's drumming	Choose a sound song	Super Sound Sequences	Row, row, row your boat	The Train Ride by June Crebbin	Which animal is hiding?	Copy my claps	All Aboard!	Train Ride
WEEK 4	Little drummer's drumming	Choose a sound song	Super Sound Sequences	Row, row, row your boat	Pants by Giles Andrea	Syllable scramble	Copy my claps	All Aboard!	Pants!
WEEK 5	Little drummer's drumming	Choose a sound song	Super Sound Sequences	If you're happy and you know it	Kitchen Disco by Clare Foges	Syllable scramble	Copy my claps	All Aboard!	Have a kitchen disco!
WEEK 6	Little drummer's drumming	Choose a sound song	Super Sound Sequences	If you're happy and you know it	Veg Patch Party by Clare Foges	Syllable scramble	Copy my claps	All Aboard!	Veg Patch Party!

The children will be learning to:
- Learn simple songs and sing from memory.
- Join in with repeated refrains in stories.
- Copy a rhythm by clapping or using an instrument.
- Repeat a rhythm by clapping or using an instrument.
- Make up our own rhythmic patterns.
- Clap the syllables in our names.
- Clap the syllables in everyday words.
- Count the syllables in words to sort objects.

★ Super Serious about Super Sounds | A Year of Super Sounds Weekly 45-minute sessions
Term / Semester 2b – Step 4

	5 mins **GAME 1**	5 mins **GAME 2**	5 mins **GAME 3**	5 mins **SONG**	5 mins **JOINING IN STORY**	5 mins **GAME 5**	5 mins **GAME 6**	5 mins **GAME 7**	Take Home Task **SUPER SOUNDS AT HOME**
WEEK 1	Pass the tambourine around	The Drummer's in the ring Loud and Quiet	Big Band Game	We're Driving in Our Car	*The cat and the rat and the hat* by Em Lymas	Magical Words game (with rhyming objects)	Noisy Dice Game (with rhyming pictures)	Musical Sounds Game (Rhyming words version)	The Cat and the Rat
WEEK 2	Pass the tambourine around	The Drummer's in the ring Loud and Quiet	Big Band Game	We're Driving in Our Car	*Oi Frog!* by Kes Gray	Magical Words game (with rhyming objects)	Noisy Dice Game (with rhyming pictures)	Musical Sounds Game (Rhyming words version)	Rhyming I Spy
WEEK 3	Pass the tambourine around	The Drummer's in the ring Loud and Quiet	Big Band Game	We're marching in our wellingtons	*Chocolate Mousse for Greedy Goose* by Julia Donaldson	Magical Words game (with rhyming objects)	Noisy Dice Game (with rhyming pictures)	Musical Sounds Game (Rhyming words version)	Yum Yum!
WEEK 4	Pass the tambourine around	The Drummer's in the ring Fast and Slow	Big Band Game	We're marching in our wellingtons	*Shark in the park* by Nick Sharratt	Magical Words game (with rhyming objects)	Bags of Fun game	Musical Sounds Game (Rhyming words version)	Shark in the park
WEEK 5	Pass the tambourine around	The Drummer's in the ring Fast and Slow	Big Band Game	I'm a pirate	*Super Duck* by Jez Alborough	Magical Words game (with rhyming objects)	Bags of Fun game	Musical Sounds Game (Rhyming words version)	Super Ducks!
WEEK 6	Pass the tambourine around	The Drummer's in the ring Fast and Slow	Big Band Game	I'm a pirate	*Go Go Pirate boat* by Katrina Charman	Magical Words game (with rhyming objects)	Bags of Fun game	Musical Sounds Game (Rhyming words version)	Rhyming with pirates

The children will be learning to:
- Hear the similarities in the first spoken sounds in words.
- Say the first spoken sounds in words.
- Find two objects beginning with the same sound from a set of objects.
- Sort objects which don't begin with the same spoken sound as others.
- Say a 4-word tongue twister from memory.
- Sort similarities and differences in letter shapes.

Super Serious about Super Sounds | A Year of Super Sounds Weekly 45-minute sessions
Term / Semester 3a – Step 5

	5 mins	5 mins	5 mins	5 mins	5 mins	5 mins	5 mins	5 mins	Take Home Task
	GAME 1	**GAME 2**	**GAME 3**	**SONG**	**JOINING IN STORY**	**GAME 5**	**GAME 6**	**GAME 7**	**SUPER SOUNDS AT HOME**
WEEK 1	Little drummer's drumming	Choose a sound song	Super Sound Sequences (More complex patterns)	This is the way we lay the bricks	*Hippo has a Hat* by Julia Donaldson and Nick Sharratt	Twizzle my tongue!	Magical Words Game (with alliterative items)	Cookie Time!	Dressing Up!
WEEK 2	Little drummer's drumming	Choose a sound song	Super Sound Sequences (More complex patterns)	This is the way we lay the bricks	*The Wonky Donkey* by Craig Smith	Twizzle my tongue!	Magical Words Game (with alliterative items)	Cookie Time!	Let's listen
WEEK 3	Little drummer's drumming	Choose a sound song	Super Sound Sequences (More complex patterns)	A sailor went to sea, sea, sea	*The Dinky Donkey* by Craig Smith	Twizzle my tongue!	Magical Words Game (with alliterative items)	Cookie Time!	Spot the difference
WEEK 4	Little drummer's drumming	Choose a sound song	Super Sound Sequences (More complex patterns)	A sailor went to sea, sea, sea	*Bathroom Boogie* by Clare Foges	Simple stories (Getting ready for bed)	Supermarket sort game	Noisy Dice Game	Bathroom Boogie
WEEK 5	Little drummer's drumming	Choose a sound song	Super Sound Sequences (More complex patterns)	Heads shoulders knees and toes	*Hooray for Fish* by Lucy Cousins	Simple stories (When I go on holiday I need)	Supermarket sort game	Noisy Dice Game	Let's look
WEEK 6	Little drummer's drumming	Choose a sound song	Super Sound Sequences (More complex patterns)	Heads shoulders knees and toes	*Pete the Cat and the Perfect Pizza Party* by Kimberly and James Dean	Simple stories (When I go to the supermarket I got)	Supermarket sort game	Noisy Dice Game	Perfect Pizza

The children will be learning to:
- Hear the similarities in the first spoken sounds in words.
- Say the first spoken sounds in words.
- Find two objects beginning with the same sound from a set of objects.
- Sort objects which don't begin with the same spoken sound as others.
- Say a 4-word tongue twister from memory.
- Sort similarities and differences in letter shapes.

super sounds

Super Serious about Super Sounds | A Year of Super Sounds Weekly 45-minute sessions
Term / Semester 3b – Step 6

	5 mins	5 mins	5 mins	5 mins	5 mins	5 mins	5 mins	5 mins	Take Home Task
	GAME 1	GAME 2	GAME 3	SONG	JOINING IN STORY	GAME 5	GAME 6	GAME 7	SUPER SOUNDS AT HOME
WEEK 1	Pass the tambourine around	Choose a sound song	Big Band Game	*1 finger 1 thumb keep moving*	*Monkey Puzzle* by Julia Donaldson	I hear with my little ear	Pirate captain says (oral blending version)	Musical Sounds Game (oral blending version)	I hear with my little ear
WEEK 2	Pass the tambourine around	Choose a sound song	Big Band Game	*1 finger 1 thumb keep moving*	*A squash and a squeez* by Julia Donaldson	I hear with my little ear	Pirate captain says (oral blending version)	Musical Sounds Game (oral blending version)	Which is it?
WEEK 3	Pass the tambourine around	Choose a sound song	Big Band Game	*Down in the Jungle*	*The Koala who could* by Rachel Bright	I hear with my little ear	Pirate captain says (oral blending version)	Musical Sounds Game (oral blending version)	Can you hear it?
WEEK 4	Pass the tambourine around	Choose a sound song	Big Band Game	*Down in the Jungle*	*The squirrels who squabbled* by Rachel Bright	What is it Game	What's the word Mr. Wolf	Musical Sounds Game (oral blending version)	What's my word?
WEEK 5	Pass the tambourine around	Choose a sound song	Big Band Game	*Here we go round the mulberry bush*	*Mrs Blackhat* by Mick and Chloe Inkpen	What is it Game	What's the word Mr. Wolf	Musical Sounds Game (oral blending version)	Let's do magic!
WEEK 6	Pass the tambourine around	Choose a sound song	Big Band Game	*Here we go round the mulberry bush*	*Mrs Blackhat and the zoom broom* by Mick and Chloe Inkpen	What is it Game	What's the word Mr. Wolf	Musical Sounds Game (oral blending version)	Flying high!

The children will be learning to:
- Hear all the separate sounds in a spoken cvc word.
- Say all the spoken sounds in a cvc word.
- Orally blend spoken sounds to say the full cvc word.
- Match orally blended words to corresponding objects / actions.
- Orally segment words to say each spoken sound separately.
- Retell a simple familiar story from memory.

Want to teach super sounds Spectacularly Weel?

Ready for Reading ONLINE!

Ready for Reading

The HIGH VALUE, ESSENTIAL Pre-Phonics training for EVERYONE working with 2, 3 and 4 year olds.

Learn even more about how to teach Super Sounds Spectacularly Well with the author, The Learning Lady!

★

What's included:

* Essential knowledge about how children learn and how Super Sounds helps them later on

* Heaps of practical top tips and suggestions

* Ideas and advice for using Super Sounds in your school or setting

We'd love you to join hundreds of practitioners just like you :)
www.learninglady.co.uk/phase-1-phonics-training

@learninglady